3/18

Praise for *Tasks Before Apps*

Monica Burns is one of the leading authorities on the effective use of educational technology. Her latest book does not disappoint, as she compels educators to be more purposeful when it comes to digital tasks. She skillfully leads readers through a thoughtful process that emphasizes a doctrine of pedagogy first, technology second. If you want to get more out of technology, then this book is for you.

—*Eric Sheninger, Senior Fellow,*
International Center for Leadership in Education

Tasks Before Apps addresses a common technology problem in education: the tendency to chase the newest apps without focusing on the learning tasks they'll be used for. This book provides a powerful tool to support teachers in meaningfully integrating technology and 21st century skills in their everyday teaching. Each chapter includes practical, developmentally appropriate examples for multiple grade levels and discusses ways to address standards while engaging students in meaningful content creation.

—*Dr. Theresa Cullen, Associate Professor,*
Jeannine Rainbolt College of Education, University of Oklahoma

Tasks Before Apps is filled with practical tools and strategies for educators. Burns guides teachers through a process of lesson design that is firmly focused on learning, as she presents opportunities to foster curiosity and classroom collaboration. This is a resource that educators can use to extend their thinking around technology integration as we strive to support students as content creators.

—*Cathy Hunt, Arts Educator, Advocate, and Advisor*
Founder of www.iPadartroom.com (@art_cathyhunt)

Tasks Before Apps provides a solid foundation for novice and veteran educators who are looking to integrate technology the right way. Dr. Burns takes readers through pedagogically sound methods that promote student success and pairs them up with appropriate digital tools. This book is a must-read for educators from all walks of life who are serious about changing the way technology enhances learning experiences.

—*Brad Currie, 2017 NASSP National Assistant Principal of the Year*

Technology evolves rapidly, and apps come and go. What doesn't change is the core of learning: wondering about the world, understanding it, and creating projects that help others understand. Burns shows, with concrete examples backed by research, how both novice and experienced teachers can energize their classrooms by integrating technology for the purpose of learning—not just for the purpose of learning tech. I wish I'd had this book when I started teaching!

—*Michael Hernandez, Apple Distinguished Educator,*
Google for Education Certified Innovator, and Lead PBS Digital Innovator

An important book with an important message, *Tasks Before Apps* articulates the importance of creation over consumption and places the student at the center of the narrative whilst emphasizing the importance of pedagogy in the "learning with technology" journey. Monica's passion for this subject comes through in her writing. A must-read for teachers.

—*Paul Hamilton, Head of Learning Technologies at MFAC, Founder of* iPad Monthly, *and author of* If I Were a Wizard *picture book and augmented-reality app*

Tasks Before Apps is a must-read for both preservice and inservice teachers working to integrate technology in their classrooms. Teachers will learn how to design meaningful tasks for students and then choose the right digital tool to support the learning, while differentiating instruction and engaging students in their learning journey.

—*Dr. Julie A. Kozisek, Professor of Education, Doane University*

Dr. Monica Burns frames her thinking in *Tasks Before Apps* in a way that offers guidance for real, meaningful technology integration in any classroom. If you're ready to take teaching and learning to the next level with technology, read this book with a team and make a plan of action now!

—*Kyle Pace, Director of Technology, Grain Valley School District*

Tasks Before Apps is a comprehensive guide to integrating technology in the classroom. Dr. Burns presents practical tools and resources while keeping student learning at the heart of technology use. As an early adopter of technology in the classroom, I have seen many teachers be lured by the use of apps and online resources without regard to the quality of the product and connection to content. This book will be a valuable resource to help our staff make connections between learning goals and the use of meaningful technology for promoting curiosity and collaboration.

—*Dr. Michele Ogden, ASCD Emerging Leader and Principal, Irvine Unified School District*

Whether you are eager to integrate even more digital tools or are feeling overwhelmed by all the apps and options, Monica Burns is here with practical, classroom-tested advice. In *Tasks Before Apps*, she wisely keeps the focus on learning goals while showing us how tech tools can scaffold and strengthen students' curiosity, collaboration, and creative potential.

—*Suzie Boss, author of* Reinventing Project-Based Learning, Real-World Projects, *and* Bringing Innovation to School

TASKS

BEFORE

APPS

To my parents, for your continued love, support, and enthusiasm for learning.

TASKS BEFORE APPS

BEFORE

APPS

DESIGNING
RIGOROUS LEARNING
IN A TECH-RICH CLASSROOM

ASCD

Alexandria, VA USA

MONICA BURNS

1703 N. Beauregard St. • Alexandria, VA 22311-1714 USA
Phone: 800-933-2723 or 703-578-9600 • Fax: 703-575-5400
Website: www.ascd.org • E-mail: member@ascd.org
Author guidelines: www.ascd.org/write

Deborah S. Delisle, *Executive Director;* Robert D. Clouse, *Managing Director, Digital Content &
Publications;* Stefani Roth, *Publisher;* Genny Ostertag, *Director, Content Acquisitions;* Allison
Scott, *Acquisitions Editor;* Julie Houtz, *Director, Book Editing & Production;* Miriam Calderone,
Editor; Masie Chong, *Graphic Designer;* Mike Kalyan, *Director, Production Services;* Barton
Matheson Willse & Worthington, *Typesetter;* Kelly Marshall, *Senior Production Specialist*

PAPERBACK ISBN: 978-1-4166-2466-0   ASCD product #118019   n10/17
PDF E-BOOK ISBN: 978-1-4166-2467-7; see Books in Print for other formats.
Quantity discounts are available: e-mail programteam@ascd.org or call 800-933-2723, ext. 5773,
or 703-575-5773. For desk copies, go to www.ascd.org/deskcopy.

Library of Congress Cataloging-in-Publication Data

Names: Burns, Monica, 1986– author.
Title: Tasks before apps : designing rigorous learning in a tech-rich classroom / Monica Burns.
Description: Alexandria, Virginia USA : ASCD, [2017] | Includes bibliographical references
    and index.
Identifiers: LCCN 2017026466 (print) | LCCN 2017037624 (ebook) | ISBN 9781416624660
    (paperback) | ISBN 9781416624677 (PDF e-book)
Subjects: LCSH: Computer-assisted instruction. | Educational technology. | Internet in
    education. | Lesson planning.
Classification: LCC LB1028.5 (ebook) | LCC LB1028.5 .B8745 2017 (print) | DDC 371.33—dc23
LC record available at https://lccn.loc.gov/2017026466

27 26 25 24 23 22 21 20 19 18   1 2 3 4 5 6 7 8 9 10 11 12

TASKS BEFORE APPS

ACKNOWLEDGMENTS

This book would not have been possible without the thousands of educators whom I have met during my travels. Their passion and enthusiasm for thinking outside the box, diving into something new, and placing the needs of their students first are common threads that bring us all together regardless of where we call home.

Thank you to the educators who share their stories within *Tasks Before Apps* and to the colleagues in my own professional learning network who have offered guidance throughout the process. Your thought-provoking conversations, quick messages, and support have had an immeasurable impact.

A final thank-you goes to ASCD and my editors Allison Scott and Miriam Calderone. Your guidance, enthusiasm, and patience shine throughout the pages of this book.

INTRODUCTION

From the day I put pencil to paper to outline each of the chapters in this book to the moment this book sits in your hands, the landscape of digital tools has changed. Technology's rapid evolution over the course of months, not years, is a reminder of how important it is to keep our goals for student learning front and center. This book was designed to put the learning first, to help you leverage the power of technology to place *tasks before apps*.

As a classroom teacher, I was continually amazed by the possibilities a new website or app offered my students. Digital tools opened up a world of content for students to access and ways for them to explore and apply the information and ideas that were once confined to their textbooks. As educators, we have the opportunity to leverage digital tools to address more than a list of objectives—to teach the transferable skills we strive to ensure that each child masters.

Tasks Before Apps was designed to help educators take traditional lesson design to the next level by providing inspiration and actionable ideas for technology integration in K–12 classrooms. This book places emphasis on three overlapping, intertwined categories: creation, curiosity, and collaboration. As students *create* a product, they dive into content, demonstrate understanding, and make a shareable creation. When we honor and cultivate *curiosity*, students explore their personal interests, wonder about the world around them, and see our time together in the classroom as relevant and purposeful. When students *collaborate*, they learn to think critically, compromise, and develop a skill set essential for success both inside and outside school.

This book outlines a way to examine your current practice and infuse tech-rich experiences to (1) turn students into creators, (2) honor students' curiosity, and (3) provide opportunities for collaboration. Although I've called out so many of my favorite digital tools throughout this book and included vignettes in which other educators share their own favorites, this book is designed to help you focus on your learning goals, design rigorous tasks, and choose the right tools for your students. It's not about the latest tablet or the fastest laptop but about designing learning experiences that use the power of technology to reach every learner. To that end, I've included forms and templates in Appendix A to support you in your planning and goal setting. (For added utility, these forms can be downloaded at http://www.ascd.org/ASCD/pdf/books/Burns2017forms.pdf. Use the password "Burns2017118019" to unlock the PDF.)

Digital tools let us capture student voice, change the way students interact with the world, and provide an audience for children of all ages. When technology is partnered with rich learning experiences in a thoughtful, purposeful manner, we can elevate traditional instructional practices to prepare students for the world of today and tomorrow.

1.

THOUGHTFUL TASK DEVELOPMENT

When I first implemented a one-to-one iPad program in my classroom, all I could think about were apps. Was there an app that could solve this problem, fix this issue, help to do this? I thought I was on the hunt for the perfect app—but when students held those tablets in their hands, I quickly learned that I was really looking for much more than a single application.

Thoughtful technology integration that places "tasks before apps" should be a goal for all teachers designing learning experiences for their students. In beginning our journey, we must start by asking, What is the task? What are our expectations for the learners in our classroom? How will we help them explore the content we are charged with teaching?

Task Development 101

In this book, the term *task* describes an experience during which students create a product that demonstrates their mastery of learning goals. As the educator in your classroom, you will determine the learning goal for students based on their needs, interests, a set curriculum, and/or local standards. With this learning goal in mind, you will identify the success criteria students must meet to show their knowledge of content, and design a learning experience accordingly. This does not need to be a one-size-fits-all task; we'll explore ways to honor student voice and choice throughout this book.

The tasks you design for students will vary based on a handful of factors, including content area, grade level, and your access to different resources. A larger task might address several learning goals and require a deep dive into content over a period of a few weeks. A smaller task might connect to a single learning goal and be completed within a daily lesson. In this chapter, my aim is to help you identify learning goals and formulate a plan for thoughtful technology integration.

Designing Rigorous Learning Tasks

As educators, we want to foster students' ability to persevere in solving challenging problems, and we can encourage this by designing tasks that facilitate deeper learning experiences. Author and educator Barbara Blackburn defines *rigor* as "creating an environment in which each student is expected to learn at high levels, in which each student is supported so he or she can learn at high levels, and each student demonstrates learning at high levels" (2013, p. 13). Teachers can maintain high expectations for students while also ensuring that supports are readily available.

Before directing students to open an app on their tablet or pull up a website on their laptop, pause to ponder the following questions:

- At the end of today's lesson, what should students understand? (*Learning goals*)
- How will I know for sure if students understand? (*Expectations*)
- What would I like students to accomplish today? (*Learning experiences*)

Without a clear answer to the first question, it is impossible to design a rigorous task. *Learning goals* help you determine *expectations* and create *learning experiences* for students. Thinking backward in this manner—identifying the learning *goals* before learning *experiences*—will help you plan for daily lessons and entire units of study.

Setting a Purpose for Learning Tasks

When we set a purpose for learning, students understand *why* they are completing a task. The *why* tells students how a learning experience in the classroom connects to the real world. With technology tools, students can reach a large audience and apply what they've learned in real-world contexts. They can record their voices as they interview an expert on climate change, create a slideshow of images from a field trip, or design a tutorial that shows other kids how to solve a long-division problem. Teachers who choose learning goals thoughtfully can connect technology to learning goals with a purpose and create learning experiences that their students view as relevant both inside and outside the classroom.

When we place tasks before apps, our priorities move front and center. Thinking of the purpose of a task rather than focusing on available apps helps us make sure students are learning skills they can use at any point in their life—even when technology changes. Using digital tools in the classroom should help students acquire skills they can use in the future with or without the current technology at hand.

Throughout this book, we'll look at the ways teachers can energize traditional learning experiences by adding relevance and purpose. We'll also examine how technology tools can help teachers reach students by differentiating tasks to address individual needs with greater ease. There are many ways teachers can use technology to unlock the potential of students who may have difficulty showing what they know in traditional ways. Students who are conversationally proficient in English and working on their writing skills can benefit from voice-to-text technology, for example, and those who need extra scaffolding might receive support from their teacher more efficiently on personal digital devices.

The tasks we develop for students can acknowledge and celebrate the changing world. As we take charge of the content we want students to learn, we can package the information into experiences that are memorable, meaningful, and transferable to other contexts.

Creating a Plan for Classroom Success

All you need is the plan, the roadmap, and the courage to press on to your destination.

—Earl Nightingale

A *learning goal* is what you want your students to understand or experience by the end of a lesson or unit. A daily lesson might have one learning goal, or a single learning goal might be addressed over the course of several lessons. A unit or month-long investigation of a topic might have several. You might use a frame like "Students will be able to . . ." (SWBAT) when composing learning goals.

Identifying your learning goals before a unit or lesson is essential. It helps you understand what your students will explore through direct instruction, supported group activities, or independent practice. Knowing your learning goals also helps you figure out what to look for when checking to make sure students demonstrate mastery, or *get it*, as you teach a lesson and review student work after a lesson is complete. A clear understanding of your learning goals also lays the foundation for thoughtful technology integration. (Visit the following website for a video overview of the SWBAT approach to designing goals: https://www.teachingchannel.org/videos/making-lesson-objectives-clear.)

A unit is composed of a set of learning goals and expectations for student understanding. In *The Understanding by Design Guide to Creating High-Quality Units*, Grant Wiggins and Jay McTighe present a curriculum-planning framework to give educators "a way of thinking purposefully about curricular planning" (2011, p. 3). Keep long-term results in mind as Wiggins and McTighe do to establish clear learning goals over the course of a unit. Identifying student expectations for a unit of study can help you integrate digital tools in a thoughtful, purposeful manner.

Educators can honor and elevate successful past practices through the thoughtful use of technology tools. Examine the goals of the unit you have in mind and determine how technology can best be used to help students create products that demonstrate their understanding. This might mean having students design interactive timelines in a high school history class, for example, or supporting students as they create tutorials for solving math problems in an elementary math classroom. Activities such as these can be threaded into existing units or learning activities.

To help develop our thinking around using technology for deeper learning experiences, I use the ACES framework, which I first presented in my 2016 book *Deeper Learning with QR Codes and Augmented Reality*. The elements of the framework are as follows:

- **Access**—Students can easily and efficiently locate content hosted online to find information, answer questions, or connect with others.
- **Curate**—Students interact with resources handpicked by their teacher that relate to course content, student interest, or the individual needs of learners.
- **Engage**—Students use technology tools to build transferable skills during hands-on learning activities that require them to create products and collaborate with others.
- **Share**—Students have an authentic audience for their learning, setting a purpose for their work and connecting their creations to the world outside the classroom.

Creating a Unit Plan

Let's first think about a unit as a whole. For example, if your goal is to have students develop an understanding of the scientific method by conducting an experiment, there are places in this unit where technology tools can elevate the experience. In this scenario, you could include a task for students to develop questions for a Skype visit with a scientist from a university lab, or use online collaborative documents to share the results of their experiment. As the facilitator of your students' learning experiences, you are thinking of the overall mission for the unit first, then working backward to integrate technology in a way that will support your end goals.

Figure 1.1 (p. 8) shows a sample unit plan using both the SWBAT sentence starter for setting goals and the ACES framework for integrating

Figure 1.1
Sample Unit Plan Using SWBAT and ACES

Unit Title: Hands-On with the Scientific Method

Learning Goals: Students will be able to
1. Distinguish the different components of the scientific method.
2. Plan an experiment by gathering information from multiple sources.
3. Conduct and document the steps of a scientific experiment.
4. Summarize their learning process using multimedia resources.

Overarching Mission: To develop an understanding of the scientific method by conducting an experiment.

Culminating Task: Students will create an e-book to share on our class blog that documents the steps they took while conducting an experiment.

Expectation: Students will complete all steps of the scientific method, use domain-specific vocabulary, and create a digital product.

Technology Integration: Digital tools will be used to
- Introduce key terms through a multimedia scavenger hunt.
- Demonstrate the scientific method in action.
- Connect with an expert through videoconferencing.
- Capture student work through images and video.
- Organize student summaries and media to create an e-book.
- Share student creations on a digital platform for a partner class to view.

Potential Tools:
- Book Creator (new for students, used last year)
- Kidblog (students have accounts/pages)
- iPad camera (one device for each group)
- Nearpod (one device each for lesson)
- Skype (use teacher-created account)

The ACES Framework: Technology will elevate this unit by helping students to
- *Access* resources by virtually connecting with an expert through a Skype call.
- *Curate* content by organizing it and supporting media into an e-book.
- *Engage* with learning by capturing hands-on experiences as they happen.
- *Share* with others by publishing an e-book on the class blog for the partner class to view.

technology tools. In developing such a plan, it is important to examine the steps students will follow when completing a task and identify where digital experiences will fall in the sequence of a unit.

Another way to think about how you will embed technology into your unit is to examine the *process* leading to task completion. In this scenario, you are thinking more generally about the mission of your unit and ways in which you can use technology to elevate student learning experiences. Brainstorming in this manner can provide a vision of where digital experiences will fall into the sequence of your unit. As you begin to think about where you are taking your students and the product they will create, you can plug in ideas along this pathway (see Figure 1.2).

The example in Figure 1.2 can be tailored to different grade levels. Students in 1st grade might explore the scientific method using terms like *prediction* instead of *hypothesis* and try out an audio tool to record their summaries; 10th graders might locate experts and address the

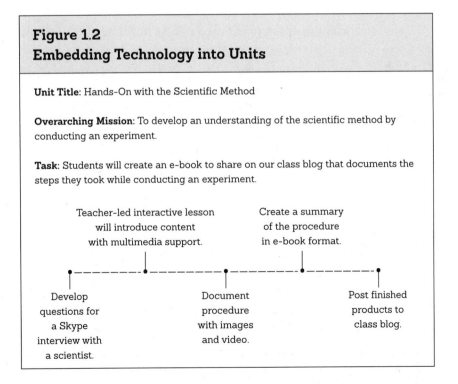

Figure 1.2
Embedding Technology into Units

Unit Title: Hands-On with the Scientific Method

Overarching Mission: To develop an understanding of the scientific method by conducting an experiment.

Task: Students will create an e-book to share on our class blog that documents the steps they took while conducting an experiment.

Teacher-led interactive lesson will introduce content with multimedia support.

Create a summary of the procedure in e-book format.

Develop questions for a Skype interview with a scientist.

Document procedure with images and video.

Post finished products to class blog.

logistics of setting up an interview in addition to developing questions to ask. Regardless of grade level, your role as the educator is to identify the learning goals, expectations, and experiences you want students to have as they interact with content.

Past Versus Present: How Technology Has Altered the Classroom Experience at Different Grade Levels

Consider the following three examples of the same content being taught in a traditional classroom and a technology-rich classroom.

Example 1

In a 1st grade classroom of the past . . . students might be asked to draw a series of simple shapes and label each one. This task might include cutting shapes out of construction paper and making a poster for display on the walls of the classroom.

In a 1st grade classroom today . . . students might be asked to snap a picture of their drawing of each shape and record themselves naming its properties and the things that make it different from other shapes. Alternatively, students can draw the shapes using an illustration tool on their devices and create a slideshow where they name each shape as it appears on the screen. Students might also take pictures of trapezoids, circles, and squares found inside and outside their classroom and arrange these on a slideshow or digital poster, carefully labeling each image. This student product could be the culmination of a two-week unit on shapes.

Example 2

In a 5th grade classroom of the past . . . students might be asked to examine rocks and minerals in a kit and take notes on what they observe during an earth science unit. They would then use their notes to write a report comparing and contrasting rocks and minerals.

In a 5th grade classroom of the present . . . students might be asked to sort through rocks and minerals in a kit, holding each one in their hand.

As they scan a QR code next to each item, they are taken to a website to view an interactive map that shows where a rock appears in nature or to watch a video showing how minerals are used in different industries. With technology, students can access information on rocks or minerals that might be hard to bring into the classroom, like diamonds or opals. Students then create a tutorial about what they've learned using a screencasting tool that includes images, text, and voice narration as the culmination of the unit. (In addition to having students complete the digital tutorial, teachers might include a virtual reality field trip to a national park during the unit or a videoconference conducted with a mineral expert two time zones away.)

Example 3

In an 11th grade classroom of the past . . . students might be asked to compose a literary essay connecting a current event to a classic piece of literature. This essay could serve as part of a portfolio of student writing samples for a college application.

In an 11th grade classroom today . . . students can examine a classic piece of literature using an app that lets them annotate as they read and access their text and notes on any device. They might research a complementary current event by gathering a variety of online sources, including articles, video clips, and images. With technology, students can create a concept map to help connect their research on a current event with textual evidence from the literature they've read. By composing their essays using an online collaborative tool, students can share their work with teachers and peers who can leave feedback using a comment tool as the writing progresses. The final essay can serve as a culminating project for a writing unit. Students can publish it online and include links to additional relevant information, videos that provide plot summaries, or images that connect to different key points in the essay. Links to students' essays could be shared on a school Twitter feed, posted in an online class forum, or connected to a QR code and displayed in the library.

All three examples described above include a culminating product of student work made possible by digital tools. Technology is used as part of the exploration of course material, creation of content, and sharing of student work. The culminating project is the result of a series of smaller tasks designed to help students master and interact with content.

Lesson Planning

Now that we've explored task development and unit planning, let's turn our attention to the planning of day-to-day lessons. The culminating project taken on by your students will be composed of a series of smaller tasks designed to help students master and interact with content. In the same way we've stepped back to think about how technology will be used at the unit level, let's examine how this might look in daily lessons.

Isolating Lessons

A unit plan can help teachers think backward and make a big-picture plan. As we shift to thinking about day-to-day instruction, we can isolate lessons to examine how technology can be used effectively in smaller bites. As you dig deeper into a unit's learning goals, you will develop a plan for the individual lessons you would like to teach.

The lesson-planning tool in Figure 1.3 has been completed to reflect a sample lesson for the unit on the scientific method presented in our discussion of unit plans. (Blank versions of the forms in Figures 1.1 and 1.3 can be found in Appendix A.) I chose the learning goal for this lesson by thinking about what I want students to accomplish, how I can set them up for success, and how I can best foster creation, curiosity, and collaboration. The technology-rich tasks students complete in daily lessons can be part of the process toward a long-term project or isolated explorations of a given learning goal.

If reexamining unit plans to integrate technology seems like a daunting task, start small by developing one- or two-day lessons that incorporate digital tools. You might decide to teach your first unit of the school year in a traditional manner and choose one or two moments to elevate the learning experience using technology. As the school year progresses, you can continue to integrate technology into existing units or revise upcoming

Figure 1.3
Sample Lesson Plan

Unit Title: Hands-On with the Scientific Method

Unit Learning Goal Addressed in Lesson: Students will be able to plan an experiment by gathering information from multiple sources.

Description of Lesson: Students will prepare questions for a scientist who conducts experiments at a university.

Direct Instruction: Introduce students to their mission of gathering information about the role of a scientist. Explain that they will create a set of questions to ask the scientist about the role of the scientific method in her everyday work. Ask students to think-pair-share in small groups with the following prompt: What will you need to know about this scientist to develop good interview questions? Collect student responses digitally through a TodaysMeet backchannel or record them on a sheet of chart paper for students to reference. Explain to students that today they are going to learn more about this scientist and her work by asking questions that connect to the scientific method.

Group Exploration: Students access web content about the scientist (via LinkedIn), her university (via the department homepage), her area of expertise (via YouTube), and the scientific method (via content from previous lesson) by scanning QR codes or clicking on a link posted in an online learning management system. Students use a shared document to brainstorm and refine their questions within their small groups. They will decide on two final questions and present them to the class.

Teacher Tasks: Locate the scientist for an interview, gather digital resources, make sure students have devices both to access content and to collaborate on a shared document, and confer with small groups to help them connect their questions to the scientific method.

The Lesson Addresses . . .
- *Creation:* Students create a list of questions and narrow it down.
- *Curiosity:* Students explore the scientist's background and her work to develop questions.
- *Collaboration:* Students work in small groups to explore resources and develop questions.

units to include more opportunities for creation and collaboration as you honor student curiosity. In this way, you can build your confidence and make connections between your current instruction and available tech resources.

Here are some examples of lessons incorporating technology across subjects and grade levels:

- **Second grade**—Students develop a how-to guide that outlines the steps for making their favorite sandwich. They use interactive sequencing tools to place the steps in order. Students first record their voices to describe the steps, then add images to their how-to guide using pictures taken with a digital device or found online.

- **Sixth grade**—Students research a career in their community and create a "day in the life" profile on this career. To prepare for interviews with community members, students first post the questions they plan on asking into a learning management system like iTunes U or Edmodo and solicit feedback from peers. When students conduct the interviews, they use a tablet to record the community members' answers.

- **Tenth grade**—Students identify and investigate a problem in their community and create an action plan to share with a governmental agency. Students use a mobile device to record footage related to the issue in question and to research potential solutions. They organize their information in a document to share with community leaders.

Whenever students are working toward an end goal, you as the teacher determine the expectations for what they will need to accomplish along the way. For example, instead of using the graphic organizer you've always used, try an interactive tool to let students customize a concept map as they collect information on their topic. Perhaps the note-taking routine you've always introduced to students might now include the use of PDFs that students can annotate with voice recordings on their digital device. The minilesson on revision that is a must for your middle schoolers? Try including an opportunity for students to jot down notes and submit their revisions to you digitally. Digital tools can transform traditional, everyday tasks into relevant, customizable learning experiences for students.

Reflecting on Lesson Planning

Taking time to reflect on the use of technology within a lesson can help you make sure the learning goal remains front and center: *tasks before apps*. The teacher planning tools at the beginning of Appendix A can aid in your planning and reflection. As artifacts of your own reflection and growth using technology in your classroom, these planning tools might spark a discussion in a professional learning community (PLC) meeting or be brought into a conversation with your administrator on your professional goals. The use of a teacher tool to reflect on your lesson provides a window into the way you are using technology in a robust and meaningful way.

You may have come across mentions of the SAMR model while exploring educational technology integration. Developed by Dr. Ruben Puentedura (2014), the SAMR model describes different ways technology can alter learning experiences in a hierarchy from *S* to *R*: *S* = *substitution*, *A* = *augmentation*, *M* = *modification*, and *R* = *redefinition*. The SAMR model can help you examine technology integration at the lesson level, allowing you to step back, conduct a pulse check, and quickly reflect on your choice of digital tools and tech-infused learning experiences for students.

Both the ACES framework and the SAMR model can be used to guide purposeful planning. Although some schools use the SAMR model to evaluate how effectively teachers use technology in the classroom, I advise against this practice. The ACES framework and the SAMR model are important tools for pushing educators' thinking beyond the surface level and can be used to facilitate conversations on thoughtful technology integration.

Checking for Understanding

One of the most powerful aspects of open-ended digital tools is that they don't require students to answer specific questions or reach a particular level to succeed. Instead, students use their knowledge of a topic, the task you have designed, and the support you offer them to create products that demonstrate their understanding. This freedom to work on a blank canvas is wonderful—for students who are prepared to jump in. It can also feel overwhelming for students who might not know exactly how to approach a tool that doesn't come with steps to follow. For this reason, among others, it is vital to check for student understanding during and across lessons. Rubrics, exemplars, checklists, and graphic organizers can all help teachers properly assess both student progress and the effectiveness of technology integration.

Rubrics

Rubrics that outline your expectations for students are appropriate for long-term projects. In *Formative Assessment and Standards-Based Grading* (2010), instruction and assessment expert Robert J. Marzano describes the development of rigorous rubrics in terms of learning goals. The first step, he writes, is to identify a set of learning goals; then, identify different levels of complexity to create a scale. The rubric in Figure 1.4, for example, shows a scale of 1 to 3 detailing the key indicators used to evaluate student work and provide specific feedback.

The example in Figure 1.4 is just that—an example. If you plan to spend a lot of time highlighting domain-specific vocabulary, your expectations for how students use this vocabulary might shift. The same is true if you are working with students who have spent very little time taking pictures or video in the past. If students have little experience with collecting media, this is not an area you will identify as success criteria. As you develop an assessment plan, you may even decide to determine the learning goals for a unit and then have the students work together to develop the criteria for success.

Rubrics allow you both to evaluate student work and to communicate expectations. Over the course of a unit, you can confer with students either formally or informally using rubrics to guide conversations. You can use this tool to make sure you have planned lessons that address your expectations for student mastery. For students, a rubric ensures you have identified all of the components you want them to master. Receiving rubrics at the outset

Figure 1.4
Sample Rubric

Unit Title: Hands-On with the Scientific Method

Task: Students will create an e-book to share on our class blog that documents the steps they took while conducting an experiment.

Learning Goals	Scale of Complexity		
	1	2	3
1. Distinguish the different components of the scientific method.	Define and explain each component in context of the experiment and demonstrate the importance of following the scientific method.	Define and explain each component and place components in sequential order.	Define components but demonstrate limited understanding of their order.
2. Plan an experiment by gathering information from multiple sources.	Develop a detailed plan for an experiment after reviewing multiple options; gather information from multiple sources and document its influence on your plan.	Develop a plan for an experiment and gather information from multiple sources.	Use a premade plan to conduct an experiment and gather information from a source.
3. Conduct and document the steps of a scientific experiment.	Conduct a complex experiment following all protocols and procedures; consider when different types of recording tools (audio, video, still image) are best suited to document learning.	Conduct an experiment, taking pictures and videos to document learning.	Conduct a simple experiment with support, taking a few pictures or videos to document learning.
4. Summarize the learning process using multimedia resources.	Summarize each step of the experiment using domain-specific vocabulary and multimedia (video and images) to illustrate concepts and elaborate on text descriptions.	Summarize each step of the experiment using multimedia supports, including video and images.	Summarize each step of the experiment using video or images.

of a unit helps to clarify for students what is expected of them and guide the direction of their projects. (For younger elementary students, consider sharing a simplified version of the rubric you plan to use to assess student work written in clear, friendly language.)

Exemplars

"What should it look like?" It's vital for students to understand what sort of shape, more or less, their product should take. An exemplar does not have to limit student creativity when used as a model. Traditionally, teachers would hold on to a piece of student writing or a student project at the end of a school year to use as an exemplar (or a nonexemplar) the next year. As we shift to incorporating digital tools into our instruction, this practice of modeling and sharing examples with students can help them not only understand expectations but also evaluate the work of others and reflect on their own progress.

You may decide to create an exemplar yourself to model expectations for students using digital tools. In the workshops I run for teachers, attendees often participate in a "digital make-and-take," where they create a product using the same tools their students have access to, with the same expectations they have set for students. Carving out time to create an exemplar will enable both you and your students to understand the direction a project will take and will help you anticipate how to address differentiation of a task. Social networks like Pinterest and Twitter also give you the option to search for models created by other educators. If locating a true exemplar is a challenge, you will want to closely model each step of creating the final product to ensure it aligns with learning goals and expectations for students.

Checklists

Teachers might choose to create a checklist rather than a rubric for a one- or two-day lesson to ensure that they have modeled all the necessary components. Checklists also help students to frame their thinking, monitor their progress on one or more tasks, and transfer the skills a teacher models to their own independent work. Checklists tend to be more quantitative than rubrics, featuring yes/no responses, and should be used as a tool to support students working independently.

Graphic Organizers

If you'd like to allow students some flexibility with their final products or you know they will need extra support along the way, you may decide to use graphic organizers, which help students plan for their work. A graphic organizer can include anything from a table where students fill in how they plan to use domain-specific vocabulary in their e-book to a T-chart that helps students plan narration to accompany images they've chosen for a slideshow.

Graphic organizers can be used digitally or on paper. In paperless classrooms, you might see students completing a graphic organizer in one web browser tab while conducting research for their project in another web browser tab. In classrooms with limited access to technology (e.g., where tablets are used only on certain days), you might find students on nontech days sketching storyboards and writing scripts for how-to videos using pencil and paper—work that ensures they're prepared when it comes time to record their videos using digital tools.

Energizing Tasks with Technology

What does it mean to *energize* a task with technology tools? Effective use of technology in the classroom goes beyond introducing a new tool to grab the attention of students. Energizing a task with technology means you are breathing life into your classroom. You have identified what your students need to know and used technology tools to make their work relevant and meaningful. You are helping students develop skills used in all facets of their lives to prepare them for a world where problem solving and communicating with digital tools is the norm. Figure 1.5 (p. 20) shows examples of how technology can energize the pursuit of different learning goals.

Figure 1.5
Examples of Energizing Lessons Through Technology

Learning Goal	Technology Integration	How the Lesson Is Energized
Classify shapes based on the number of sides.	A virtual geoboard app (http://catalog.mathlearningcenter.org/apps/geoboard) lets students draw their own polygons. Students label the different shapes based on the number of sides.	Students can • Create endless shapes. • Manipulate figures • Color-code instantly. • Collect images of their work.
Compare and contrast two characters in a novel.	Students use a concept-mapping program (http://popplet.com) to create a map of traits for each character in the novel. They color-code and connect different sections of the web to show similarities and differences.	Students can • Customize their graphic organizers. • Add to the map as their thinking evolves.
Describe the steps for a "how-to" piece of informational writing.	Students take pictures or video to document each step of their how-to process and write a paragraph explaining the process using domain-specific vocabulary. Students then create a movie using a digital program (https://spark.adobe.com/about/video) that sets the pictures or videos they took to a narration of the explanatory paragraph.	Students can • Choose how to document their learning. • Design a tangible product that demonstrates their learning. • Create a video that can be shared with an audience.

The Takeaway

To make student learning meaningful, we need to

- Honor students as creators of content who apply what they learn in a relevant manner.
- Listen to students' interests as we push them to wonder.
- Develop a community of active, supportive learners.

Now it's time to dive into the world of creation, curiosity, and collaboration with both tasks *and* tech in mind!

2.

CREATION: DEMONSTRATING UNDERSTANDING EVERY DAY

Two students are sitting in the corner of a classroom. They've just finished reading chapter books in literature circles and are leaning over a tablet together. The students are choosing images and adding text to the screen, pausing to record their voices, taking turns speaking into the microphone. The book trailer these students create in pairs will be shared on the school library's Twitter feed and included on an interactive bulletin board.

How can you support students as they create products that demonstrate their understanding of a topic? With digital tools, students can access text, images, and videos in a matter of clicks.

Students are now consuming and interacting with content throughout the school day, with or without the guidance of peers, parents, and educators.

To push students beyond merely consuming and interacting, we need to give them opportunities to *create*. Content creation is not a novel idea in education. Students have recited speeches, performed plays, written biography reports, and conducted science experiments for decades. In this chapter, we'll explore how technology tools can elevate and energize traditional product-creation strategies.

Approaches to Product Creation in Schools

Long before tablets, laptops, or computer labs became fixtures in schools, students documented their learning by creating products. Giving students the power to create gets their wheels spinning about a topic, helps them make connections, and provides relevance to their work. In his popular TED Talk, Sir Ken Robinson (2006) notes that "creativity now is as important in education as literacy, and we should treat it with the same status." How often do we give students an opportunity to demonstrate their understanding by exploring content in hands-on learning experiences? Are we giving students a sense of purpose for and ownership over their learning?

Many schools strive for true project-based learning (PBL), with teachers incorporating proven PBL strategies into their instruction. One suite of such strategies is the Buck Institute's Gold Standard PBL model, which provides a framework for designing problem-based tasks that address key knowledge, understanding, and success skills (Larmer & Mergendoller, 2015). Teachers can develop tasks that provide opportunities for students to create a public product that honors their voice and choice. Creation of a public product is an essential component of PBL, as is the establishment of an authentic audience. With technology tools, we can provide rich experiences for student creators and connect them with a range of audiences to set a purpose for their work.

Lorin W. Anderson and colleagues (2000) developed a revised cognitive domain of Bloom's taxonomy that highlights the importance of creation in classrooms. Viewed as the highest level in the taxonomy, *creating* requires students to have a solid foundation of *understanding* to design and create a product that demonstrates the *synthesis* of what they know. Although digital tools are not required to create a product, technology used purposefully can elevate and energize learning experiences.

The Partnership for 21st Century Learning (2015) outlines a framework for learning that includes creativity and innovation. It suggests three main categories or steps of creative work: *think creatively*, *work creatively with others*, and *implement innovations*. The last category—implement innovations—is key for our discussion on creating tech-rich learning environments, encompassing how students will "act on creative ideas to make a tangible and useful contribution."

How Creating Products Using Technology Helps Students Develop Transferable Skills

Transferable skills are those that can be applied outside of the classroom, across disciplines, and in multiple contexts. When students have the ability to successfully solve problems, manage their time, and communicate clearly with others, they are prepared to confront any number of situations—and digital tools support the development of these skills during classroom lessons.

In *5 Myths About Classroom Technology* (2016), author Matt Renwick argues that "we struggle with technology in today's schools because *we aren't sure when it is necessary and when it is just nice*" (p. 2). When digital tools are used to elevate traditional learning experiences, students have opportunities to apply their learning in relevant contexts; they build the problem-solving skills necessary to maneuver in digital spaces and prepare for a world where a handful of innovations can completely transform an industry. From brand marketing to daily e-mail correspondence, every aspect of most professions has experienced sudden changes requiring the application of transferable skills that students can strengthen through the purposeful use of technology in school.

Creating a product requires students to synthesize the information they have explored during a unit of study and demonstrate their understanding in a tangible manner. Students can create a range of products to demonstrate mastery of the learning goal(s) you have identified for a daily lesson or a month-long unit. There is no one right answer as to what students should create for any given unit of study. A myriad of factors will influence your decisions.

Dioramas, scale models, book reports: when we spoke about student projects in the past, we usually envisioned static things that you could touch with your hands. Digital tools now let students create dynamic products that include a range of media, allow for instructional differentiation, and promote curiosity and collaboration. Advances in technology allow students to build, sketch, and write as they explore new concepts and demonstrate their learning.

Characteristics of Digital Creation Tools

Digital creation tools such as online programs and mobile apps give students the space to tell a story of their learning, providing them with a blank canvas on which to add text, audio, images, and more to create a digital end product. There is no single best type of digital resource for students to use. There are many ways to document learning, and the types of tools your students use should vary over the course of a school year. See Figure 2.1 for descriptions and notable examples of different types of digital products; Figure 2.2 (p. 26) shows the purpose of various features common to many digital resources.

Consumption, Creation, and Critical Thinking

Our students are avid consumers of content. Over the course of a single day, they might watch a video clip, listen to an interview, scroll through an article, or click a link on social media. Digital tools have transformed the way we teach students to be critical thinkers about the information they encounter. With devices in their hands, students of all ages can access material of all kinds with ease. As educators, we must help students navigate the

Figure 2.1
Types of Digital Student Products

Type	Description	Examples
E-book	A collection of digital pages that may include text, images, hyperlinks, or narration	• Book Creator http://bookcreator.com • iBooks Author https://www.apple.com/ibooks-author/
Slideshow	Series of images played like a movie with music and/or narration	• Google Slides https://www.google.com/slides/about • Keynote http://www.apple.com/keynote/
Movie	Video recording that may include still images, animation, music, or voice recording	• Spark Video https://spark.adobe.com • iMovie http://www.apple.com/imovie/
Screencast	Captures the movements on your screen to create a movie with voice, images, and animation	• Explain Everything https://explaineverything.com • Screencast-O-Matic https://screencast-o-matic.com
Audio recording	Captures sounds, voice, or music to create podcasts or music recordings	• GarageBand http://www.apple.com/ios/garageband/ • Soundtrap https://www.soundtrap.com
Poster creator	Provides space where users combine images and text	• Spark Post https://spark.adobe.com • Canva https://www.canva.com
Concept map	Diagram with ideas linked together that may include text, audio, or images	• Popplet http://popplet.com • BrainPOP Make-a-Map https://www.brainpop.com
Word processing	Text-based document that may include hyperlinks or images	• Google Docs https://www.google.com/docs/about/ • Pages http://www.apple.com/pages/
Website creator	Publishing tool incorporating text, images, video, and/or hyperlinks designed to be shared online	• Spark Page https://spark.adobe.com • Sway https://sway.com
Scale model	Provides a space for students to build a virtual model; some tools connect to 3D printers.	• Minecraft https://minecraft.net/ • Tinkercad https://www.tinkercad.com

Figure 2.2
Features and Purposes of Different Creation Tools

Feature	Purpose	Examples
Text	To add words, phrases, or sentences	• Adding a caption to a photo • Including a series of paragraphs on a website to introduce a new idea
Audio	To record audio or import an audio file	• Recording narration for an e-book • Interviewing an expert for a podcast
Video	To record video or import a video file	• Filming a welcome video for a website • Creating a stop-motion animation
Images	To capture a still image or import an image file	• Adding pictures to a how-to e-book demonstrating steps in a process • Snapping photographs during a field trip to feature in a slideshow
Graphics	To add icons or shapes like rectangles, arrows, or talk bubbles	• Using an arrow graphic to point to a part of a picture on a web page • Adding talk bubbles to the pages of a digital comic book
Links	To connect readers of a digital product with other web-hosted content	• Adding links to a digital poster so readers can click to learn more about a topic • Curating links to resources for a web page about a food drive
Music	To add music or import a music file	• Including thematically appropriate music in a slideshow • Recording music that captures the theme or tone of a novel

information they come across as consumers while also empowering them to create content of their own. Indeed, by creating products that demonstrate their understanding, students become smarter consumers; they are better able to assess the value of any website, video, or image that pops up on their screen because they have had experience in the roles of both creator and consumer. See Figure 2.3 for a few examples of consumption versus creation using digital tools.

Figure 2.3
Digital Content:
Consumption Versus Creation

Consumption	Creation
• Watching a video • Reading an article • Listening to a podcast • Skimming search engine results	• Publishing a blog post • Snapping pictures for a slideshow • Making videos of observations • Posting on social media

Ryan Orilio, a technology coordinator from New Hartford, New York, recommends PhotoCard, a mobile app that lets users create postcards to send to friends and family. Ryan designed a project where students used the PhotoCard app to create a postcard from the point of view of a historical figure. They had to conduct research to learn about the person and address the postcard to someone who played an important role in his or her life. With Ryan's task, students learn about a period in history while using digital tools to create a product that demonstrates their understanding.

Creation in Action

Students can demonstrate their understanding by creating a tangible and shareable product. Here are some examples of how students at different grade levels might create digital products as they explore different topics.

First Grade

Students explore the characteristics of a community by taking a walking tour of the neighborhood around their school or making a few stops with their teacher on a field trip. With their tablets in hand, students snap pictures of buildings, signs, and objects that represent the way the community works. When they return to the classroom, students open up the pictures they took in an app like Book Creator. They select a picture for each page, record narration, and add descriptive text. They might each create one interactive page to contribute to a class e-book or fill multiple pages for their own e-book on communities. The final creation can be shared with peers in a special celebration and added to the class's digital library.

In this example, technology elevates the students' learning experience. At the beginning of the creation process, they are gathering media with digital tools, focused and engaged on their walking tour because there is a clear purpose for their learning. Instead of cutting pictures out of magazines and gluing them to construction paper, students use technology to capture their own images—adding both immediacy and personal agency to the task.

Fifth Grade

Students investigate sustainable farming across three different subject areas: an ecosystem unit in science, an ancient civilization unit in social studies, and a persuasive writing unit in English. During their research, students take a position on the best way to farm in a chosen ecosystem and create a public service announcement to convince their audience. Students collect images to create a slideshow using the tool Shadow Puppet and write a speech they then record as narration. The slideshows are shared with a museum curator who is planning an exhibit on ancient civilizations; she posts the student creations on the exhibit's website.

In this example, students are working on a cross-curricular project to research and create a multimedia product. With digital tools, students can access resources, organize the information they collect, and create a shareable product. Technology further elevates this learning experience by connecting students to an authentic audience.

Ninth Grade

Students design a new playground for a nearby day-care center using their understanding of math and physics as well as research into building codes. After conducting a needs assessment, measuring the space, and building a model, they present their findings on a website created with Spark Page. Students share links to their pages with builders in the community to solicit feedback or with the child care center as inspiration for a future design project.

In this example, technology helps students gather information, develop a plan, and document their thinking on a website. Digital tools elevate this learning experience by allowing students to build scale models and present their thinking in a shareable online space. Students are also able to connect with community members both during the design process and when they are ready to share their final product.

Deciding on a Final Product

When should students make a website? When is a movie a better choice? Should you give students many options and have them pick what to make? It depends on the activity and the learning goal. In some cases, many different tools can work. Consider our 1st grade example of the neighborhood walk, for instance. If the learning goal is to have students gather information and describe a place, you might add creating a slideshow or designing a poster to the process. If an app that suits the activity comes preloaded on school tablets, it makes sense to make use of it.

Here's an example of how to decide on a final product regardless of subject or grade level. Let's say you want students to create a personal narrative sharing a special moment from their lives that includes select story elements you've modeled in numerous minilessons. Students might compose this personal narrative in writing on a piece of paper, or they might create a digital product that incorporates such story elements as dialogue or figurative language. Figure 2.4 (p. 30) shows some of the reasons you might choose one digital creation over another as you prepare students for this activity; Figure 2.5 (p. 31) shows the potential positive results of each choice.

Kristi Meeuwse teaches kindergarten in a one-to-one iPad classroom in Charleston, South Carolina. Her students document their thinking by creating math journals on their iPads. They take pictures of the math manipulatives on their desks and screenshots of their work inside other math apps, then record their learning in an e-book using Book Creator. With this tool, students can combine pictures, screenshots, illustrations, and their voices to create a math journal that documents what they have learned over the course of the school year.

Guiding Questions for Choosing Tools

Here are some questions to consider when deciding on a digital tool for students to use:

- Will students need to record video or take pictures to complete the activity?
- Does the tool let students layer features on top of one another (e.g., text on top of images)?
- Can the tool help students create a final product that is shareable with an authentic audience?
- Does the tool supply images, or will students need to provide their own?

Figure 2.4
Reasons for Selecting Different Digital Tools to Complete the Same Task

Task: Compose a personal narrative sharing a special moment from your life.

E-book	Slideshow	Website
Description: Students combine text, video, and images on multiple pages to tell the story of a special moment.	**Description**: Students combine still images and narration to tell the story of a special moment.	**Description**: Students compose text and choose media to support the retelling of a special moment.
Reason for choosing: You might choose an e-book for this project if you want to differentiate the lesson; some student e-books can be text-heavy, while others focus more on video. If your school has tablets available, an e-book is a great choice to connect your students' work with an audience by uploading the finished e-books to devices used by students throughout the school community.	**Reason for choosing**: You might choose a slideshow for this project if you want students to focus on literary elements as opposed to writing conventions. Because a slideshow requires plenty of planning, creating one can boost the confidence of students who struggle as writers by giving them a space to record their voice as they focus on plot, theme, or characters.	**Reason for choosing**: You might choose a website if there are a lot of supporting materials like videos or images for students to organize in one place. A website gives students space to curate content that supports their writing. Links to the websites students create can also be shared easily; students can post them in a discussion forum to receive feedback from peers or attach the link to a QR code for an interactive bulletin board.

Your Role as Teacher

With or without digital tools, creation in the classroom provides opportunities for students to explore a topic collaboratively or independently. Your role as teacher during the creative process may include

- Monitoring student progress and needs through regular check-ins with groups and individuals.
- Intervening when necessary by providing additional support, resources, or guidance.
- Adjusting your plans to address teachable moments, student questions, or tangents worth exploring.

Figure 2.5
Potential Positive Results of Different Technology Choices

When Students . . .	They Become . . .	And Understand . . .
Make an e-book	Published authors	The importance of text structure and content organization
Create a website	Stronger evaluators of online content	How to curate resources related to a given topic
Design a slideshow	Media-savvy producers	How to sequence events in a narrative or timeline

Students who are making a product to demonstrate their understanding have already listened to a minilesson, participated in a hands-on activity, or discussed their reflections from a field trip, but this doesn't mean their learning stops when it's time to create. Students who are designing a scale model on Minecraft or preparing for a podcast with GarageBand are immersed in a deep learning experience that will spark more questions and further investigation. A checklist or simple set of instructions can help students get started with an open-ended creation tool, providing them with a foundation for their work and clarifying exactly what they must do to effectively demonstrate understanding. As students examine exemplars and nonexemplars and dive into a task, you may decide to invite them into the process of setting expectations for their own creations.

Cathy Yenca is a math teacher from Austin, Texas, who shares checklists with students when they are creating in groups so that they know exactly what they have to do to accomplish their goals and who is responsible for each component of the task. Cathy's students then use other digital tools to represent their thinking and create a product that demonstrates their understanding. To learn more, visit http://www.mathycathy.com/blog/2014/05/students-use-book-creator-to-author-mathematics-part-1.

Autonomy and Choice in Product Creation

Student creators are motivated by a sense of autonomy and choice, which are also essential components of task development. Designing tasks that allow students to create a product they are interested in and excited about is crucial for keeping them engaged. Every teacher can design lessons that honor students' autonomy while making sure the learning objective stays front and center. As lead learner in your classroom, you have an opportunity to curate the appropriate digital tools for different tasks based on student input.

To illustrate, let's examine how teachers of different grade levels and content areas might provide students with choice when working on the same culminating project: creating a short video for the whole class to watch.

Kindergarten

Students work with partners to record their voices over digital pictures to create a slideshow about a character from a favorite book. In September, everyone tries the same tool—one the teacher has modeled and helped students use. If this task is completed in February, the teacher might ask students to choose between two tools they've been presented with over the course of the year to describe a character from a book they've read. Because your students are now familiar with more tools, they can choose to create an interactive poster, a movie, or a slideshow for their reading response. Giving students a choice helps them take ownership of their learning.

Sixth Grade

Students in a 6th grade classroom work in small groups to film and edit a movie documenting a special event in the school community. In September, the teacher encourages each group to use a tool that the students have had experience with or that has a short learning curve. If this task is completed in February, the teacher might have each group choose a tool from a list of three moviemaking options, providing time for students to discuss and arrive at a joint decision. At this point in the school year, students in each group work together to address the task. The teacher monitors and intervenes if students need help using the moviemaking tool they've chosen.

Twelfth Grade

High school seniors create a video that outlines the challenges of navigating the school website and offers a plan for redesigning it. The teacher introduces a few tech options for video creation or encourages students to propose a tool that will get the job done. Students' project proposals should explain how the tool they choose helps them address the task and complete the project on time. If students choose a digital tool you are not familiar with, you can point them to tutorials online if they get stuck or have a question you can't answer.

Student choice is about honoring student interests and providing opportunities for students to explore their passions with your support. You can thoughtfully guide students and connect their actions to learning goals. The purpose for using a specific tool should be clear from the start of the project, and you as the teacher can decide how many choices you present to students.

Supporting the Creation Process

The shift from traditional student creations (reports, posters, dioramas) to digital products (videos, interactive maps, online portfolios) requires us to change how we think about our work in the classroom. Learning goals are still front and center, of course, and mastery of content remains a priority, but assessment of student creations is so much more than grading a final project. The learning journey students take is key, and they need support from their peers and teachers throughout the creation process.

Although the process of creation may take a few turns along the way, it is essential to establish a plan for ensuring student success. Preparing to support students as they complete a project requires teachers to think through the steps students will need to take both with and without digital tools. Figure 2.6 (p. 34) shows examples of potential steps for creating two different types of products to demonstrate knowledge of two different topics. The steps you decide on should be tailored to the task, available tools, and your expectations for students.

The creation process for any task offers opportunities for differentiation and scaffolding. Each step students take to create a product may require different supports, and you may need to increase or decrease the level of scaffolding for certain tasks or individual students over the course of the project. At the outset of a task, a template (as opposed to a strict guide) can support and inspire students as they work—perhaps presented

Figure 2.6
Examples of Steps in the Creation Process

Task	Product	Steps
Students will create a public service announcement to teach peers how to prepare for a hurricane.	Screencast	• Sketch a storyboard. • Write dialogue. • Collect images. • Practice animation. • Record the screencast.
Students will design a landing page for the new exhibit on Susan B. Anthony at the local museum.	Website	• Conduct research. • Interview a museum docent. • Gather primary source documents. • Locate or create video content. • Write copy for the website.

Tammy Musiowsky, an ASCD Emerging Leader and elementary school teacher in Singapore, teaches her students about the colors, functions, and meanings of signs and symbols as part of a unit on personal expression. Students then create their own personal symbols using what they learned. First they develop an idea on paper, then they practice using Google Drawing to create the symbol. When they're finished, they share their creations with classmates, exchange feedback, and, if necessary, revise their design. Students come away understanding that peer feedback helps them create a stronger final product.

as a digital file that students can access on their devices and alter with their own text and media. For example, you might create an outline for your students' writing. They can drag and drop their own information into the template and then format it to meet the needs of their project.

Graphic organizers can also support students as they create with technology. You might decide to give students a few options of graphic organizers to choose from. For example, concept maps are particularly fluid and let students organize their thinking in a way that makes sense to them. Students might also sketch out a storyboard to ensure their movie or slideshow has a clear sequence. On paper, students can use graphic organizers to prepare for digital learning experiences—especially useful in schools that do not have regular access to technology but use digital tools one day a week or a few months a year. When using graphic organizers on a tablet or web browser, students can organize information and then transfer it to their final product. Figure 2.7 shows a few examples of possible graphic organizers.

Figure 2.7
Graphic Organizer Examples

Task: Create an e-book that documents the life cycle of a butterfly.

What vocabulary words will you include in your book?

1. _____

2. _____

3. _____

Task: Create a slideshow that presents information on a notable figure in history.

What types of pictures will you search for?

1. _____

2. _____

3. _____

Task: Create a model of an eighth wonder of the world.

What characteristics are found in the seven wonders of the world?

1. _____

2. _____

3. _____

When I host workshops for teachers, one of the questions I often receive is "How much time should I spend showing my kids how an app or website works?" Although the answer will vary depending on your students' age group and the specific tool you are using, here is my rule of thumb: spend just one to three minutes going over the basics, then give students a minute to explore the tool and try out the features before applying it to a task. If you think your students may have questions while they use the tool, let two or three students practice using the new website or mobile app you've chosen for this task before you introduce it to the whole class. These students can then be called upon by their peers to answer questions as they all work on the activity.

Allocating the Right Amount of Time for Creation

The amount of time you allocate for students to complete a project will inevitably influence the creation process. It is important to make sure you reserve the necessary amount of time to accomplish the goals you have set for students. In most cases, the time you have available during a unit of study is predetermined and will dictate just how deeply you can take students on a learning journey. Having a clear plan for the creation process will ensure that extra minutes aren't wasted and you can dedicate as much time as possible to turning students into creators. The following examples show creative processes of different lengths at different grade levels.

Kindergarten

This activity occurs in a single day, in the middle of a weeks-long unit on shapes. Students read an interactive storybook about shapes on their tablets. With a partner, they then classify shapes in an app by examining the number of sides of various polygons. Students can combine the shapes and name them, discussing each one with their partner. They label each shape and point out the number of sides using the annotation or drawing option within the app. Students then take a screenshot and save their work for their teacher to review. This screenshot is the end goal of the day's activity and helps students prepare for making an e-book about shapes later in the year.

Sixth Grade

This activity occurs over multiple days during a unit of study in an English language arts class. For the activity, students are asked to compare and contrast two characters in a novel they're reading in class using a concept map. To prepare students for the concept map they'll be asked to complete, the teacher models gathering supporting evidence and introduces students to the idea of organizing their thinking using an interactive space.

Instead of using one single type of graphic organizer, students manipulate the shapes in an interactive program to add different ideas. They color-code each box in their organizers and revisit the map as they finish each chapter of the novel.

Students share links to their concept maps with the teacher so he or she can peek in at their creations over the course of the unit. Creating the map could be the culminating product of the unit or one step in the process of a different student creation, such as a book trailer to persuade other students to read the novel.

Twelfth Grade

This activity occurs over several days or even weeks, depending on the established learning goals. Students use a camera app on their devices to snap pictures showing the effects of a weather system on the growth of plants in a community garden. Back in the classroom, students conduct research on weather systems, write a paragraph describing the evidence they've collected in each picture, and incorporate the text into a slideshow. This tangible finished product documents students' ability to write informational text supported by media and can even be shared at a town hall meeting.

Each of these examples illustrates the process that leads up to a final student product. The creation process requires

1. A clear plan influenced by established learning goals and expectations.
2. Differentiation and scaffolding to address individual student needs.
3. An understanding of how long it will take to complete the project.

Assessing Student Creations

Assessing the process of product creation is not about assigning a letter grade; rather, it is about understanding how best to support students as they work individually or in small groups. You are helping students design, develop, and create a final product using support materials and strategic interventions. Whatever rubric you've traditionally used for assessing student products can remain the same in a technology-infused classroom—with a few additions.

For example, let's imagine your students are completing a piece of persuasive writing. Whether their final product is an essay stapled to a bulletin board or a video played for the school board, the content and core process remain essentially the same: students should hook their audience, state an opinion, use facts to support their position, and include a call to action. However, when using digital tools, the expectations for *creativity* and *clarity* are different.

Assessing Creativity

Creativity might seem subjective and thus immune to assessment, but there are measurable creativity goals students can be asked to meet, and these goals should be addressed explicitly during a unit. For example, if your students are completing a project involving music, you can explore as a class the different ways music influences an audience's perception of an issue. You can establish an expectation for students to choose music for their project that supports their intended tone. (If you don't discuss how the characteristics of music influence a listener's perceptions, then you should not hold students accountable for the music they choose.)

Assessing Clarity

Assessment of clarity is often connected to assessment of mechanics, from writing grade level–appropriate sentences to using punctuation correctly. When using digital tools, you might assess such matters as clarity of voice if there is narration involved, for example, or the navigability of a website design. Again, you should assess only the skills you have introduced and discussed with students (e.g., how to slow down their voices and speak clearly into a microphone).

The Big Picture

When you introduce digital tools into everyday lessons and existing units, take a step back to think about the final product you're asking students to create. How will you instruct them during the creation process? Are your learning goals front and center? Have you placed *tasks before apps*?

As you examine the scope and sequence of learning experiences over the course of the school year, decide where technology-rich activities—including opportunities for creation—can elevate traditional instructional goals. With digital tools, both small everyday activities and culminating projects can provide opportunities for students to create shareable products that demonstrate understanding of core concepts. In the next chapter, we will explore how to connect student work to authentic audiences while honoring student interests—two essential components of creating with a purpose.

3.

CURIOSITY: PROMOTING LIFELONG LEARNING IN THE CLASSROOM

What if . . . ? I wonder . . . ? Could we . . . ? Does this . . . ? Curious children are critical thinkers: they examine the world around them closely and aren't satisfied with simple answers. These students dig deeper into their interests to uncover the secrets behind the *why* in their everyday lives. Curious children become curious adults who problem-solve, discover solutions, and innovate. Unfortunately, curiosity often gets lost in the classroom, buried under our best intentions of meeting curriculum goals. As educators, our role is to set students up for success in a world full of unknowns. To this end, we must help them to cultivate confidence, critical thinking skills, and a sense of wonder—skills that are transferable to the world of today and of tomorrow.

Think back to your own experiences as a learner. A field trip to the planetarium, an assembly with a favorite author, a volcano model erupting in science class: these moments in our own lives are far more memorable than most classroom lectures or slideshow presentations. For our students to truly become wonderers, investigators, and innovators, we must honor their interests as we spark their curiosity.

The Paramount Importance of Curiosity

A curious student who can imagine multiple solutions to a problem is equipped to innovate when presented with challenges both inside and outside the classroom. In his book *The Global Achievement Gap* (2008), Tony Wagner names curiosity as one of the seven skills students need to thrive in a rapidly changing world, as it allows them to think outside the box and solve problems in new ways. As students explore their interests and move through content with a passionate teacher by their side, they become actively engaged in learning. Placing value on student engagement—what literacy expert Patricia Vitale-Reilly describes as "the act of being . . . passionate, hardy, persistent, thoughtful, committed, and connected to [one's] work" (2015, p. xiii)—is an essential component of honoring curiosity.

Curious students become critical thinkers who identify research topics and read between the lines. They examine their world closely and ask questions big and small. The Center for Media Literacy defines *media literacy* as "the ability to access, analyze, evaluate and create media in a variety of forms" (n.d.). Curiosity is essential in a world where students are presented with a volume of seemingly endless content to consume in a variety of formats. Students must have the confidence to analyze and evaluate as well as the drive to think deeply as one of their questions leads to another.

You can help students start developing a mindset of questioning and curiosity on the very first day of school. Just as you might spend a few weeks on routines and procedures, take the time early on to encourage students to share their interests or wonderings about the world. Then, throughout the year, incorporate activities in class where students share wonderings or pose questions they'd like to find answers to through their own exploration.

Although many students aren't shy when it comes to sharing their interests, others will need your help finding their passions. When I work with teachers throughout the United States, I love leading kindergarten students in discussions and listening to their unapologetic lists of questions and wonderings. That sense of curiosity and urge to ask questions can feel lost as you move up the grade levels. For several years, I taught in a 5th grade classroom where students often looked to their neighbors before asking a question, concerned that they would be judged for expressing curiosity. Digital tools can help you cultivate a classroom community where judgment is suspended and students are free to search for answers to their questions both independently and collaboratively.

How Technology Furthers Curiosity

Maria has her tablet in hand as she walks toward the classroom library. She's on the hunt for a new book and looking to try a new genre. There is a Roald Dahl book peeking out of a bin, and the author's name sounds familiar to Maria. Looking down at her device, she types "Roald Dahl" into Amazon to pull up a list of his other books. She notices Matilda *and remembers how much she loved reading that book last year. Maria flips the book over and sees a QR code placed on the back of the book by her teacher. She scans the QR code, and a book trailer made by one of her classmates pops up on her screen. Maria watches the 30-second clip and then makes her way back to her seat. Ready to start reading, Maria is convinced she'll enjoy* Charlie and the Chocolate Factory *as she opens the book to the first page.*

In a tech-friendly classroom, students are encouraged to be curious. Their rewards come from learning new things, mastering a skill, increasing their knowledge base, and finding solutions to their problems.

Our goal on the journey of thoughtful technology integration is to take the best practices of the past to the next level with digital tools. We want to build on the foundation of traditional tasks to empower students as wonderers and answer-seekers. As students inquire about matters both on their own and with our guidance, we can help them come to see tablets, smartphones, and computers as portals to an entire world of innovative problem solving: virtual reality (VR) experiences provoke questions, online search tools bring answers to our fingertips, and videos show how classroom skills are applied in the real world.

Think about the soft-spoken students in your class who are hesitant to raise a hand during a discussion or pose a question to their peers. Thanks to technology, they can now pick up a VR headset like the low-cost Google Cardboard and be transported to Machu Picchu using a tool like Nearpod's VR content for classrooms. Students can jot down a few questions—Who lived here? What happened to this civilization? What did they eat living on a mountaintop?—and then use a voice-to-text tool to input each question into a search engine on their tablets. When they tap one of the links that pops up on the screen, they can listen to an archaeologist explain what life was like for the Inca people living in the region we now call Peru. This experience not only teaches students a great deal about the culture of the Inca but also hones curiosity by suggesting further questions: How do you become an archaeologist? What tools do archaeologists use to research a civilization? Just how long would it take to get to Peru from where I live?

Don Goble, a multimedia educator in St. Louis, has chronicled his work with students in his e-book *Six-Word Story, Six Unique Shots: Enhancing Writing Through Multimedia* (2014; available as a free download at http://apple.co/1OhAA93). He uses a six-word story to help students practice media literacy and to engage them in problem solving. Don's six-word story model can be used across the content areas. When finished, students can publish their work in an online space that allows them to connect with an authentic audience.

Curiosity in Action

Here are just a few examples that illustrate how student curiosity can be honored and cultivated through tech-friendly classroom activities across grade levels.

Second Grade

Students take part in a discovery walk in their community, using tablets to snap pictures of signs, street art, and building structures. Swiping across their screens, students each choose one image to spark a research question. This image will set the stage for interviews with community members and a multimedia presentation in which students will use voice to tell the story of their surroundings. The culminating project addresses the unit's overall question: How do the spaces in our community affect the way people work together?

This activity honors students' interest in their own community, allowing them voice and choice in the direction of their research, and can connect across multiple subjects (e.g., English language arts and social studies). Students can take the activity further by creating an e-book that discusses a related topic, such as the intersecting roles of people and places in their neighborhoods.

Seventh Grade

Students choose an area in their school that needs a redesign. They collect and analyze survey data using Google Forms, measure and map out the space using Sketchpad, and develop a budget using a spreadsheet tool like Numbers. The project addresses the unit's overall question: How can we redesign a space to meet the goals of a client while accounting for logistical constraints?

This activity can help spark students' curiosity for future careers as project managers, architects, or interior designers. It also connects students to the spaces they inhabit in school each day. The details of the activity will vary, as always, according to your learning goals. For example, if one goal is to incorporate effective research skills, students might be introduced to relevant strategies beforehand and expected to use them.

Twelfth Grade

Students explore different industries connected to their passions (e.g., film, sports, app development). As part of a cross-curricular activity for economics, civics, and statistics classes, students decide how to invest in public companies as part of an investment club. Given a set amount of funds, they research the backgrounds of different businesses, weigh ethical issues, and create plans for making short- and long-term investments. Their project culminates in a multimedia presentation via Skype to an expert in the industry they've chosen to investigate and a visit from a local financial advisor. The project addresses the overall question, How do investors navigate ethical issues within an industry and decide which companies to include in their portfolios?

This activity encourages students to discover something new about an industry they are interested in while addressing standards-aligned learning goals across subject areas. Learning doesn't have to suffer when you thoughtfully integrate experiences that connect to student passions.

Dr. Samantha Dias-Lacy, an elementary educator from Long Island, New York, has her students work together using LittleBits (http://littlebits.cc)—small electronic building blocks that can be attached together—to create vehicles equipped to withstand the weather in various ecosystems. Instead of listening to a lecture or watching a movie on ecosystems, students take part in an engaging, hands-on, collaborative project.

Interest Surveys

A simple interest survey can help you decide in what direction to take a unit or how to group students together. Three of my favorite tools for conducting these surveys are Google Forms, which lets teachers choose the type of questions they would like to post (e.g., a rating scale, check boxes, or open-ended questions); Kahoot, which lets teachers project questions that students must quickly respond to while a clock counts down and music plays; and Nearpod, which lets teachers embed a poll or short-answer question in the middle of a presentation's slide deck. After conducting an interest survey, be sure to conduct an analysis of student responses using a form like the one in Figure 3.1 (p. 46; see Appendix A for a blank version).

In addition to surveys, everyday observations can provide a window into student interests. Showing a video to students or giving them time to discover the features of a new creation tool can add to the number of questions students pose to you or their classmates. Although you might show a

---

Figure 3.1
Sample Survey Analysis Form

Unit Title: Rock Cycle

Survey Questions:
1. Which of the following places would you most like to visit: the Grand Canyon, Mount Rushmore, or Monument Valley?
2. What do you already know about how rocks are formed?
3. What questions do you have about how rocks are formed?

Results: Students showed interest in all of the national parks and had questions about the different colors of rocks.

How will I incorporate this information into my unit? Group students according to the parks they're most interested in.

How will I use technology to further student interests? Use the National Parks app to develop a virtual scavenger hunt; take students on a virtual field trip using Google Earth.

---

short video to students with a set purpose in mind, keep your eyes and ears open. While students are watching a clip on a new topic, notice which parts spark questions or leave a puzzled look on students' faces. You can leverage their curiosity about these subjects in future lessons.

Differentiation and Student Curiosity

It is essential to provide students with multiple ways to demonstrate their understanding. To maintain a classroom where curiosity thrives, it's important to give students the space and tools they need to address the essential elements of a task through a variety of media. Workflow solutions like Seesaw: The Learning Journal, Google Classroom, and Edmodo all allow teachers to decide which students will be linked to particular math problems, for example, or receive specific reading passages in their in-boxes. Getting "just-right" resources in the hands of students—a key element of differentiation—is simpler with technology tools.

As you gauge students' levels of interest in different topics, you may decide to investigate which tools they would like to try out. Providing different options to your class shows that you value students' interests and curiosity about technology. Ask your students questions such as the following:

- Who wants to become a better moviemaker?
- Would you like to create a product that incorporates music?
- Who would like to explore graphic design tools?
- Would you like the world to see your project?

The following are some examples of differentiation in the service of furthering student curiosity (see Figure 3.2 for an abbreviated version).

Kindergarten

Students are asked to create an "All About Me" presentation. Using digital tools, they create a narrated slideshow featuring photographs and drawings. Some students are ready to add text to the screen to caption each slide, while others rely on their voices to tell a story or music to set the tone.

Figure 3.2
Examples of Activities That Honor Student Choice

Activity	Student Choice	Type of Product
Create an "All About Me" slideshow to introduce yourself to classmates.	Students can • Include images of their choice. • Choose their own colors and themes. • Decide on the sequence of slides.	Slideshow
Design a tutorial to show steps in a science experiment.	Students can • Use pictures they've captured themselves. • Choose which experiment to feature.	Tutorial
Document an important moment in the life of a historical figure.	Students can • Select the topic. • Include media of their choice in their reports. • Choose how to present the final product.	Website

To ensure that students follow their interests, they are free to use images of their choice, pick their own highlighting colors, and decide on the order of the slides.

This activity gives students the opportunity to choose the direction of their final product based on their interest and ability to demonstrate understanding. The learning goals remain intact, but students have plenty of agency with their final creation.

Third Grade

Students are asked to create a tutorial that shows the steps for a science experiment. With digital tools, they can create a screencast incorporating images from their experiment, text that highlights key words, animation to demonstrate movement, and a voice recording. To differentiate this task for students, the teacher distributes a list of key vocabulary words or an outline to follow for students in need of extra support. To maintain student interest, the teacher lets students choose which experiment to document or assigns them a topic based on interests expressed in a survey.

Rich Perry, an English teacher from Merrick, New York, uses the robot Sphero (http://www.sphero.com) to help students gain a deeper understanding of classic literature. For example, when studying *The Grapes of Wrath,* Rich uses Sphero to help students simulate the characters' journey to California. Rich is able to leverage the sense of wonder students have when they control a robot in the context of learning goals.

This activity promotes students' natural curiosity by letting them pick a science experiment to conduct and document. There is also room in this activity to provide students with any scaffolding they may need.

Eighth Grade

Students are asked to publish an informational text featuring multimedia to document an important moment in the life of a historical figure. The final reports are presented either as documents with hyperlinks or QR codes, or as e-books with embedded video clips. In their final product, students might include images with captions they've written or embed a stop-motion movie they've created to bring their reports to life.

This activity lets students choose from a list of people to study and decide how to present their research.

Students have the flexibility to use a tool they have interest in exploring while creating a product that addresses learning goals.

Cultivating a Wonder Mindset

A *wonder mindset* is a way of thinking that values curiosity, asking questions, and searching for answers. In a classroom that cultivates such a mindset, teachers should be comfortable using phrases like these:

- I'm not sure of the answer.
- Where can we go to look for more information?
- There might be more than one answer to your question.
- Should we look for a video or an article to help us understand better?
- Who might be an expert on this topic?
- Let's post our question on social media.

Cultivating a wonder mindset means acting as a "guide on the side" in the classroom, facilitating and supporting learning but giving students space to explore their curiosity. As the lead learner in your classroom, it is also your job to model what curiosity looks like during authentic moments throughout the school day. Don't be afraid to pause and add a question to a wonder wall when teaching a minilesson, for example, or to think aloud so students can learn from your own curiosity and process of finding answers to questions. When students see you pull up a YouTube video to find the answer to a science question or use Google to search for a map to find directions before a field trip, they'll start to better understand how they themselves can use digital tools to fulfill their curiosity.

In classrooms where curiosity is valued and celebrated, students pose questions and search for answers, during both teachable moments and long-term inquiries. You might have students place questions they have on sticky notes at the front of the classroom at the start or the end of the day or period—or, using technology, students can submit questions via e-mail or to a discussion thread.

As students search out answers to their questions during lessons, teachers can guide them as researchers, model how to think critically as they conduct searches, and demonstrate how to evaluate potential answers as they pose questions in online spaces.

Students need to understand the difference between questions with simple factual answers and those that require a deeper dive. This can happen as they examine information from multiple sources, evaluate sources for bias, and dismiss unreliable information. Here are some examples of simple versus deep-dive questions in different grades:

- **First grade**—*Simple:* How much rain fell last summer? *Deep dive:* Why does it rain more in one state than in another?
- **Fourth grade**—*Simple:* What year did Arizona become a state? *Deep dive:* Why did Arizona gain statehood after the 13 colonies?
- **Eleventh grade**—*Simple:* What country is Jane Austen from? *Deep dive:* What factors in Jane Austen's life influenced the themes of her novels?

When examining these two types of questions, it can be useful to give students exemplars and nonexemplars. Modeling your thought process as you search for answers can benefit students at any age. Let them watch as you walk them through your search, clearly labeling your questions as either *simple* or *deep dive* and explaining why.

A Personal Example

As a 5th grade teacher, I helped create a curriculum for my grade level that integrated different subject areas into our magnet theme of environmental stewardship. When my students were ready to conduct research for an informational writing task, I was right there learning beside them. Their topics ranged from vermicomposting to wind farms, and I knew next to nothing about any of them.

My mission was to help students develop the skills they needed to locate information and to apply what they knew about informational writing to a topic they were interested in. Conducting research would have been challenging without our class set of iPad tablets: instead of giving students the freedom to explore their own interests, I would have had to limit their research topics based on available classroom or library resources.

My students' final products combined a variety of media, including both traditional and digital text features. During the unit, we focused on how to navigate the Internet to find credible information, how to use images to illustrate our writing, and how to organize content in a clear and logical way. Practicing these skills helped students become more critical creators *and* consumers of content. See Figure 3.3 for examples of how to tie different student interests to the same preexisting goal using tech-infused activities.

Figure 3.3
Same Goal, Different Interests

Learning goal: Students will identify how climate influences the economy of different regions.

Student Interest	Possible Activity	Possible Tasks Integrating Technology
Rainforests	Create a public service announcement demonstrating how the economy of a country is affected by deforestation.	• Interview a biologist via Skype. • Collect local news articles posted online. • Locate media to include in the public service announcement. • Use video software to design the public service announcement.
Planet Earth series	Create a website that provides an overview of the natural resources in a region of your choice.	• View clips from *Planet Earth* on YouTube. • Research a specific region. • Collect information on natural resources in the region. • Curate and present findings on a web-based platform.
Soccer	Create a business plan for a new sports arena that accounts for the effects of the climate on building materials, ticket sales, and transportation to and from events.	• Research the climate of a region online. • Learn about stadium features related to weather. • Use a computer program to design a plan that takes into account a variety of climate-related factors.

Evolving Curiosities

Students' passions, interests, and wonderings will evolve over the school year, and a good way to ensure learners remain curious in the classroom is to alter the learning opportunities you present to them. For example, suppose you are exploring a unit on ecosystems and focusing on coral reefs when a popular movie centered on Mount Everest comes out. To sustain student interest, you might consider shifting the focus of your lessons to the differences between abiotic and biotic factors of the tundra instead of a marine biome. Or, if your students are learning about fiction genres when a book about wizards becomes a best seller, you might incorporate mentor texts that feature magic and fantasy instead of the mystery or science fiction texts you used last year.

Sparking Student Curiosity

Often, students don't ask questions in class because they simply don't know where to start. In addition to thinking aloud and demonstrating your own process of wondering, you can spark students' curiosity about a topic by providing them with inspiring content. The following are some examples of ways to spark questions from students at different grade levels:

- **Third grade**—Play the first two minutes of a selection from a documentary on deciduous forests. Have students choose one animal featured in the video clip and guide them to ask questions on specific characteristics such as diet and habitat.
- **Seventh grade**—Show students a movie trailer from an adaptation of a book or genre they will explore before starting a text. Students can develop questions about the characters or events shown in the teaser.
- **Tenth grade**—Share an online news article about a new theme park with students before starting a new unit in physics class. Ask students to come up with questions they might ask a developer about the process of design and construction.

Embracing Wonderings

Embracing change in your classroom is an important part of creating a learning environment that fosters curiosity and creativity. Demonstrating flexibility means honoring teachable moments and understanding that the pathways to learning aren't always linear.

Teachable moments happen every day. A student asks a question that could alter the course of a discussion, or an unexpected event takes place in the community that must be addressed: these are moments to seize as opportunities for student learning. Imagine, for example, that you are teaching a unit on the Vietnam War when a student asks what it felt like to be drafted. After class, you might contact a local veterans' organization and ask if any Vietnam vets would be willing to talk to your students. Or let's say students who are studying author bias ask why the author of an article neglected to include multiple perspectives; you might choose to incorporate technology here by locating the author on Twitter and relaying the students' question.

Wondering Activities

A few weeks before kicking off a new unit, dedicate time within your lesson for a wondering activity to get your students' wheels spinning and to collect information. For example, if you are planning to start a unit on nutrition, pose a series of questions to students such as "What is your favorite healthy snack?" and "Where do you go to figure out if a food is good for you?" Gathering this information will help you honor students' natural curiosity about a topic as you prepare tasks aligned to learning goals.

In addition to organized activities focused on gathering information on student interests, you can create a culture in your classroom where students are encouraged to ask questions and investigate topics that spark their curiosity. For example, you might create a classroom environment where students know when it is permitted to open up a web browser on their laptops or pull out a smartphone to find the answer to a quick question, or when it's OK to jump up and scan a QR code that has been posted on a bulletin board or placed in a classroom library.

Authentic Audiences and Curiosity

Digital tools give students seemingly unlimited access to information to consume and a wide range of places to share the content they create. When technology is integrated purposefully into instruction, students can take on the world. Authentic audiences provide students with a sense of ownership and an opportunity to wonder and learn about the world around them. When students know who will see their work, they take ownership of it because a clear purpose has been set. Figure 3.4 shows two examples of student wonderings related to learning goals, creative projects for addressing them, and potential authentic audiences for the final products.

There are different types of audiences students can access when presenting their creative products. I use the terms *local* and *global* to distinguish two different categories. Examples of local audiences are

Figure 3.4
Authentic Audiences for Student Products
Related to Student Wonderings

Learning Goal	Student Wondering	Activity	Audience
SWBAT determine the volume of a rectangular prism and the perimeter of quadrilaterals.	How can we grow the most tomatoes in the small space of our school garden?	Create a model for a tomato garden on school grounds. Determine what supplies you will need to complete the construction.	Students will share the diagrams they create in a virtual simulation at the next town hall meeting to make a case for funding supplies.
SWBAT write a biography that includes traditional features of the genre.	Are there any famous people from our town?	Choose a person from the community of some renown. Create an interactive poster highlighting his or her achievements.	Students will share the interactive posters they create in a new exhibit at the local historical society.

those found at schoolwide assemblies, Parent Night exhibits, and presentations to the school board; global audiences extend outside the walls of your school building and into this world. Students can reach global audiences by publishing e-books, posting to social media, or videoconferencing with faraway schools. Connecting students to a global audience shows them how their work in school applies to the world outside their classroom.

Establishing an audience early on when students are working on a task is crucial, as it helps them to focus on the needs of a particular group. For example, you might decide to have students explore how to evaluate primary source documents by having them examine photographs at a museum. They can develop discussion questions to post in a new exhibit on the Industrial Revolution or in an online space that features these primary sources from this period in history. Students will have to interact with their audience—the museum curators—to find out their goals for the exhibition, locate primary source documents, and decide which artifacts are the best fit for this installation.

Here are some examples showing how students can connect with audiences for projects in different subject areas:

- **First grade**—Students research the best solution for keeping the sidewalks safe after a snowfall. They investigate weather systems and different types of substances that melt snow. They share their findings in a presentation to building staff members to help them make decisions for wintertime.
- **Fourth grade**—Students create an award for best science fiction novel. They develop assessment criteria, read a selection of books, and create videos promoting the book of their choice. Students make their announcements at a special event at the local library that is livestreamed to community members watching at home.
- **Eleventh grade**—Students develop a new logo for a local company. They must determine the goals of the organization, learn about its mission and history, and conduct research on similar groups. After designing the logo, students write a summary of their work and present the logo and the thinking behind it to the company.

In a world where learners of all ages are presented with content to evaluate, cultivating a sense of curiosity in students is more important than ever. Not only must students now analyze information at an unprecedented rate, but they also hold the tools to help them explore their world like never before. Designing tasks that require students to explore their own interests and understand how to search for answers to questions can help students become innovative, inquisitive, lifelong learners.

4.

COLLABORATION: WORKING TOGETHER WITH DIGITAL TOOLS

When students collaborate with one another in class, they participate in experiences that ask them to speak, listen, and apply their learning authentically. As educators, we want our students to be collaborators—to know how to communicate effectively, compromise, and work together to demonstrate their understanding.

Outside the classroom, students collaborate all the time, whether it's working with teammates to win a soccer game or perfecting a new song with a band. As educators, we have an obligation to prepare students for collaboration in professional contexts as well. Think of your students several years down the road: Avery might pursue a career in engineering where she needs to work with a team to develop a faster way to filter water; Isaac might enter the world of sales, where he strategizes with his colleagues, meets with potential clients, and solicits feedback from a mentor; Maya might go into health care, where she manages a team of physician assistants, listens to their concerns, and works with small teams to address quarterly goals. Avery, Isaac, and Maya can all benefit in their chosen fields from collaboration skills developed through authentic learning experiences.

In his book *Too Big to Know*, Harvard researcher David Weinberger asserts that "the smartest person in the room is the room itself: the network that joins the people and ideas in the room, and connects to those outside of it" (2011). Providing students with opportunities to collaborate is just as important as giving them time to practice solving math problems or reading independently. Students who have opportunities to collaborate learn how to navigate a world where they must communicate their ideas through various channels. If students become accustomed to receiving feedback from classmates, they will be better prepared to solicit feedback from colleagues in the future.

Born more than 100 years before the debut of Facebook and Twitter, Vygotsky (1978) chronicled how learning is a social experience. Students who collaborate aren't merely sitting together completing the same worksheet; they are engaged in stating opinions, posing questions, and elaborating on the ideas of others. When students have opportunities to work together, they understand the power of leveraging different skill sets to solve problems.

We want students to see collaborative experiences as opportunities to try something new with the support of their peers. Both state and national standards have emphasized the importance of speaking and listening in the context of collaboration. Indeed, the first standard on the list of anchor standards for speaking and listening under the Common Core notes that students must "prepare for and participate effectively in a range of conversations and collaborations with diverse partners, building on others' ideas and expressing their own clearly and persuasively" (National Governors

Association Center for Best Practices & Council of Chief State School Officers, 2010).

Students need to understand how to collaborate using digital tools—to problem-solve and exchange feedback with partners as they consume, create, and interact with content. Although there are times when placing a device in the hands of each student is the right choice for a lesson, other times you'll want students to share devices so that they can practice their collaboration skills. Collaboration is an essential component of effective teaching and learning that translates to everyday experiences and innovations.

Remote, Role-Based, and Shared-Screen Collaboration

In a tech-friendly classroom, collaboration using digital tools can take different forms: remote, role-based, and shared-screen (see Figure 4.1, p. 60). Ideally, students will have experience with all three types over the course of a school year as deemed fit by grade level, subject area, and access to digital devices.

Remote Collaboration

Students working remotely use individual devices connected by a shared document or learning management system. They might collaborate by logging on at the same time and using a chat box or webcam to communicate, or by updating a collaborative document at their own pace. Here are some examples of remote collaboration across grade levels:

- **Third grade**—A group of students brainstorms ideas for a math tutorial on a shared online graphic organizer using the Padlet platform.
- **Sixth grade**—As students conduct research on the respiratory system, they add interesting facts (with links to the original source) to a shared document. The students collect their research in Google Docs and share it through Google Classroom.
- **Tenth grade**—Students write introductions for their literary essays comparing *The Hunger Games* to a current event. They post them to the Edmodo learning management system, where students can review their peers' work and exchange feedback.

Figure 4.1
Three Types of Collaboration

Type	Definition	Example
Remote collaboration	Students work on individual devices to contribute to a single, shared creation.	Students log in to a web-based tool to add content to a slide deck in a collaborative document. The students might be sitting next to each other in class using separate devices or working from their respective homes after school. The final creation will include a handful of slides to which all students have contributed content and feedback.
Role-based collaboration	Students work on individual devices to complete assigned tasks for a group project.	Students are tasked with creating a slideshow. In groups of four, they decide what type of images to include and discuss their target audience. Then, one student takes pictures, two students prepare the narration, and the fourth student chooses music and additional media tailored to their target audience. The students take on their individual roles and communicate with their fellow group members during the process to create a single final product.
Shared-screen collaboration	Students work together in pairs to complete a task using one device.	A pair of students uses a single tablet or laptop to complete an activity. The students sit side by side, leaning over the device as they discuss their task, share ideas, and compromise. Students take turns capturing media and adding text to the final product.

In each of these examples, students can collaborate no matter how close to or far from one another they happen to be. Tools that let students work in the same virtual space by logging in with a username or through a special link are perfect for remote collaboration.

Role-Based Collaboration

In this collaborative model, students take on different roles as they work together to complete an activity. They may select their roles themselves, determine roles as a group, or have roles assigned by a teacher.

If students are breaking down a larger activity into smaller tasks and assigning roles as a group, you will want to model the process for your class, including how best to communicate with others. In role-based collaboration, students work on their own devices to complete individual tasks while communicating back and forth with peers before ultimately coming together to construct a final product. Here are some examples of role-based collaboration across grade levels:

- **First grade**—In groups of four, students create a slideshow that explains the differences among rectangles, triangles, and circles. Two students take pictures of shapes around the classroom while the other two group members draw shapes on their tablets using the Drawing with Carl app. The students then work together to arrange all their pictures into a slideshow on a single device using the Shadow Puppet Edu app.
- **Fourth grade**—In groups of three, students create an e-book featuring facts and opinions about endangered species using the Book Creator mobile app. One student writes a fact, another writes an opinion, and a third organizes the writing and records their voices for narration. For this activity, students might conduct research on their own devices and write their facts and opinions in a tool like Evernote before transferring them to the final product.
- **Eleventh grade**—In groups of four, students create a proposal for a new traffic light outside the school building. One student researches similar proposals, another interviews the local director of transportation, the third interviews the district superintendent, and the fourth takes the lead in drafting the proposal. Students use Skype to conduct interviews and Microsoft OneDrive to share documents and combine their findings into one final product.

In each of these examples, students take on roles but are not working in isolation. They have a common goal, are accountable to their group, and take the lead on a particular aspect of a group task. As students use technology to gather and share information with their groups, they can leverage the ease of access and connectivity granted by digital tools.

Shared-Screen Collaboration

The shared-screen collaboration model has students working together, usually in pairs, to complete an activity using a single device. Depending on the activity and the type of devices available, up to four students might share a single screen. Students work side by side, taking turns contributing and discussing their next steps. Here are some examples of shared-screen collaboration across grade levels:

- **Kindergarten**—Students work together on a tablet to record their voices telling a story over a slideshow using the Spark Video app. They take turns recording the narration and discuss what images to use in the slideshow.
- **Fifth grade**—Groups of four students record a podcast discussing the theme of a novel. All group members decide on questions and come to the recording session ready to talk about the book. Students use Soundtrap to record and edit their podcasts.
- **Eighth grade**—Students use a single device to record themselves in front of a green screen image of a coral reef using the Green Screen app by Do Ink. After working side by side to edit the footage in iMovie, they share their final product with the rest of the school in an Earth Day presentation.

Shared-screen collaborations are ideal for schools where there are only a handful of devices. However, even if you have a device for every student, you can still create opportunities for students to share screens as a way to practice sharing, compromising, and communicating with their peers.

Collaboration in Classrooms with Different Technology Profiles

There are so many wonderful things about one-to-one classrooms, where each student has his or her very own device. Although classrooms with only a few devices to share may seem to be operating at a deficit, collaborating on a single device can powerfully elevate traditional lessons. Three common technology profiles for classrooms include bring your own device (BYOD), mixed devices, and few devices.

Bring Your Own Device

Commonly referred to as BYOD, this type of classroom allows students to use their own personal devices during the school day. Many schools provide a list of preferred devices and the kinds of apps or extensions students will need to have preloaded on their devices before coming to school. Some schools set up profiles for students' devices and configure them for the school or district network. In BYOD environments, teachers must put tasks before apps because students may be using a variety of different programs to achieve the same learning goal. When designing collaborative learning experiences for use in BYOD classrooms, teachers must make sure these tasks can be accomplished using every student's device. Most Google apps, for instance, can be opened on Chromebook laptops, PCs, Mac computers, and smartphones.

Mixed Devices

Most schools have a mix of technology available to students and teachers. It's common to find a computer lab, a cart with tablets for students to share within their grade level, and laptops available in the media center that teachers can sign out for a day at a time. Access to multiple devices allows you to design tasks that leverage the power of different programs and tools, since students might not have access to the same devices every day.

Few Devices

In classrooms with just a few tablets or a couple of computers in the corner, it might seem like a challenge to create whole-class activities that incorporate technology. Collaboration is a natural fit for classrooms where students don't have their own devices, whatever the grade level. In classrooms with younger students, you might focus exclusively on shared-screen activities: students can come together in pairs or small groups to record their voices, arrange images on the screen, or tell stories using a single device. In classrooms with older students, you might use the handful

Robert Kalman, a middle school computer technology teacher from New Jersey, has his students use Bloxels— a hands-on, collaborative creation tool designed specifically for students—to design their own video games. This activity addresses not only the design process but also precoding concepts. Robert's students work in groups to define a game concept, brainstorm features, and create prototypes using Bloxels gameboards, cubes, and the Bloxels Builder app (http://www.bloxelsbuilder. com) on classroom devices. The students test out one another's creations and exchange feedback. They walk away with a renewed appreciation for physical and digital tools, an understanding that success is possible only when one considers the needs of others, and an expanded appreciation of video games as interactive storytelling platforms.

of devices you have to give students an opportunity to check in on a remote collaboration project or locate material for a class assignment as part of a role-based collaboration activity.

Setting Expectations for Collaboration

When we shift our emphasis from independent to collaborative work, we have an extra layer of expectations to communicate to students. A variety of factors will influence the expectations you have for collaborative tasks in your classroom. Establishing a plan for collaboration that addresses assigning student roles, managing groups, and monitoring participation is essential.

Assigning Roles

Whether students are working with their own devices or sharing a screen, they should know the role they play in completing a task. It is up to you whether to assign roles or have students assign them; teachers might assign roles to younger students (e.g., researcher, writer, recorder) and allow students who are experienced collaborators to come up with and take on roles themselves. Regardless of the approach, students should understand and be able to articulate how they are contributing to a task. To ensure this, you might ask students to outline their roles and create a to-do list at the beginning of a project.

Managing Groups

Expert groups can eliminate some of the anxiety associated with introducing students to new technology. An expert group is a small segment of your class—think 4 or 5 of a class of 30—who have spent extra hands-on time with a digital tool. You might ask students to volunteer for this role or pick one student from each small group in your class as a representative.

These students can then dedicate more time to exploring the new technology to become "experts" who support their peers as they dive into a new digital tool.

Monitoring Participation

When students work in small groups or pairs, it can be a challenge to monitor their contributions. Technology tools can help you keep tabs on student participation by checking in on student work efficiently. For example, you might decide to have students send you a daily or weekly status report to update you on what's happening in their group. The report could be a sentence-long summary or a more involved plan with actionable steps. This type of check-in is a great way for students to address questions or concerns to teachers directly. Another option is to have students create video reflections or send exit slips during the course of a long-term collaborative task. However you decide to monitor participation in your classroom, you will want to model this workflow for students.

Promoting Digital Citizenship Through Collaboration

Collaborative activities provide the perfect opportunity to introduce students of all ages to the concept of digital citizenship. Both inside and outside the classroom, students will have to work together and communicate using digital tools. Students with strong digital citizenship skills understand how to navigate the Internet, evaluate online sources, and communicate effectively on virtual platforms; they use digital channels to gather, share, and discuss information.

Developing Social Media Skills

Social media platforms like Facebook, Twitter, and Instagram can bring people together from all walks of life. When used strategically, these platforms can connect students with potential collaborators and contributors and offer them plenty of room to share their creations. Promoting digital citizenship through collaboration involves teaching students how to comment on posts, curate material, and share information with others through social media. Figure 4.2 shows examples of collaborative tasks addressing each of these skills.

The following scenarios show how students can practice digital citizenship skills while pursuing curriculum goals. (For more detailed information on aligning goals to use of technology in the classroom, see Common Sense Media's K–12 digital citizenship curriculum at https://www.commonsense media.org/educators/digital-citizenship.)

- **Second grade**—Students compose one-sentence responses to a read-aloud book. On a class Twitter feed, the teacher posts the student responses and tags the author of the book. Alternatively, students can type their responses using a tool like Seesaw, and the teacher can copy and paste them into tweets.

- **Sixth grade**—Students read an article on the solar system that the teacher locates on the current events website Newsela. They write two questions they have about the article and post them in a discussion thread on the class's Schoology page.

- **Eleventh grade**—Students read a blog post on a topic related to a social studies unit on civic engagement, then find an article about the same topic online and respond to a post in the article's comments thread. Students who are taking a position in their comments must include a link to a source that supports their argument.

Figure 4.2
Sample Tasks for Promoting Social Media Skills

Skill	Description	Sample Task
Commenting	Adding a response to a post or discussion	Students review a video made by a classmate and leave a comment describing one thing they learned from watching the video.
Curating	Researching, evaluating, and choosing resources to share online	Students search for online articles related to the unit topic by searching the Twitter feeds of experts in the field.
Sharing	Posting a curated resource or a personal product online	Students craft reactions to their classroom reading in the form of social media posts or tweets.

Before posting any student work or photographs online, make sure parents or guardians have granted permission; many districts have standard photo release forms that can be used. If permission is withheld, or if you aren't comfortable taking students into social media spaces, consider using discussion boards in learning management systems like iTunes U, Google Classroom, and Edmodo to help students practice their social media skills.

Transforming Traditional Tasks to Address Social Media Skills

Teachers can transform traditional tasks to cultivate digital citizenship skills. Although we may create experiences for older students to actually navigate the tools of the moment, all students can benefit from learning the transferable, appropriate behaviors for interacting in digital spaces. Here are a few examples across grade levels:

- **Kindergarten**—Students sit in a circle and share what their favorite vegetable is. They practice listening attentively, building on their classmates' opinions, and disagreeing respectfully. This activity gives students practice demonstrating how they value the opinion of others. Students will be able to apply these skills in the future, when they read comments online and consider whether to chime in with their own thoughts.
- **Fifth grade**—After watching a video tutorial about a new problem-solving strategy, students share their opinions about it in a discussion thread. They ask questions about the strategy and suggest ways to improve the tutorial. With this activity, students practice how to interact with and provide constructive criticism about other people's content—skills they'll be able to apply in the future when they exchange feedback with others online.
- **Eleventh grade**—Students review the comments posted on an online article from a popular news source, brainstorming with a partner ways to reword the ones that are not respectful. This activity helps students practice identifying exemplars and nonexemplars of digital citizenship and evaluate the comments of others.

Collaboration in today's classrooms needs to mean more than group projects. Integrating activities that ask students to comment, curate, and share information adds relevance to their learning and lays the foundation for smooth online collaborations beyond the classroom. Figure 4.3 shows further examples of how to transform traditional collaborative tasks to address core social media skills.

Practicing Giving and Receiving Feedback

The following classroom activities can help students engage in productive feedback loops, practicing giving and receiving comments. Even as students work on independent projects, they can collaborate with peers through a feedback cycle.

- **First grade**—Students post videos of their work using the digital portfolio tool Seesaw and comment on one another's videos, noting something they liked about them.

Figure 4.3
Examples of Tasks Transformed to Address Social Media Skills

Traditional Task	Social Media Skill	Transformed Task
Students discuss the books they've read during the year.	Commenting	Students post reviews of books they've read on an online platform using reviews posted on Amazon as exemplars and nonexemplars for how to leave a comment about a book. They read one another's reviews before choosing a new book to read.
Students look through a selection of research materials picked out by their teacher.	Curating	Students create annotated lists of links to resources they find as they research information online and share them with peers.
Students write a five-paragraph essay on a topic related to their social studies unit.	Sharing	Students create a 30-second movie that sums up their argument and uses images and icons to represent information. They post the videos on a school-hosted page and share links to their videos on social media.

- **Fifth grade**—Students share links to their work in a discussion thread in the Edmodo learning management system, where they leave one another *glows* (positive comments) and *grows* (constructive criticism).
- **Eleventh grade**—Students share their work in a collaborative online document for classmates to review. They give and receive comments with actionable suggestions throughout the document.

Students should feel comfortable posting comments on a collaborative document or reviewing work that has been shared with them electronically. Helping them develop the right tone and setting expectations is all part of this process.

Using Technology to Collaborate with Global Partners

Digital tools make the logistics of connecting with faraway people for learning experiences easier than ever. The standards of the International Society for Technology in Education (2016) even include the following expectation: "Students use digital tools to broaden their perspectives and enrich their learning by collaborating with others and working effectively in teams locally and globally." (For more information, visit http://www.iste.org/standards.)

Connecting virtually with peers in classrooms abroad helps students practice such skills as preparing for a meeting; participating in a discussion; soliciting, giving, and receiving feedback; and navigating different cultures. Students will continue to use these transferable skills long after they leave your classroom.

You don't need to have a friend who teaches far away to facilitate this kind of remote collaboration. There are social networks teeming with educators looking to expand the four walls of their classrooms. You might participate in a Twitter chat with someone who is teaching a similar topic and ask him or her to collaborate on a project with your class, or you may

Third grade teacher Stephanie Suter used Buncee—an interactive storytelling tool that includes options like adding images and animation—to help students publish and share personal narratives as part of their Writer's Workshop. Stephanie's students chunked their text and made revisions as they published their work. Using this tool, students were able to record their voices and add them to their digital creations and easily share their work with the world.

meet another teacher at a conference who is eager to connect students via videoconferencing. Thanks to social networks, it's also possible to locate and get in touch with former colleagues or education school classmates who might show an interest in collaborating. If you are using a particular tool with students, another option is to contact the company and see if its staff knows of any educators who might want to collaborate using the company's online platform, mobile app, or device.

Figure 4.4 shows some examples of how to collaborate with classrooms far and wide to meet mutual learning goals.

Planning for Global Collaborations

The process of connecting with another classroom requires more than opening up videoconferencing software and finding the best angle for the webcam. Before working with remote partners or reaching out to experts via videoconference, students and educators can create a plan to take into account the following aspects of global collaboration:

Figure 4.4
Examples of Using Global Collaborations to Meet Learning Goals

Task	Collaborative Partners	Connection Strategies
Design an e-book for the school library that describes the systems of the body.	Two 5th grade classes in different states	Students in both classes exchange feedback via videoconferencing after reviewing one another's work. The students post messages on a group discussion board to share resources as they develop their e-books.
Create a slideshow that shows the effects of weather on everyday life.	A 3rd grade class in Ottawa, Canada, and a 7th grade class in Brisbane, Australia	Students in both classes take pictures of and record audio narration about weather events over the course of a school year. The 7th graders organize both classes' images into a slideshow that explores the similarities and differences between the weather in their respective cities.

- **Conduct research.** Students should learn about the person or people with whom they'll be videoconferencing. If they are interviewing an expert, they might first pay a quick visit to the expert's website or LinkedIn profile. If they are collaborating with a class in another country, they might watch a video of what life is like in that part of the world.
- **Prepare to ask questions.** Students should draft initial questions, potential follow-up questions, and some backup questions to ask in case the conversation stalls. They might even role-play the interview beforehand.
- **Decide on the tool to use.** Choose the type of videoconferencing tool you want to use, and make sure it is compatible with the devices in your classroom as well as those on the other end of the conversation. You may consider scheduling a run-through beforehand to make sure everything works just right.

Following the videoconference, students should pause to reflect on the experience. They can discuss with their peers what went well and what they could do differently next time. Here are some examples of scenarios across grade levels following all of the above steps:

- **First grade**—Students writing an ABC book on endangered species develop questions and interview a zoologist, pet store owner, or veterinarian to learn about different animals. They conduct an interview with the expert using Skype on a class computer. After they are finished with their ABC book, the students share their creations with a class in a different state, also using Skype.
- **Fourth grade**—Students learning about fractions develop questions and interview a pastry chef, food truck owner, or cafeteria employee to see how fractions influence recipes. In small groups, students prepare questions and connect with their expert using Google Hangouts. After they are finished exploring fractions with the expert, students create an infographic that represents their findings and share their summary with another 4th grade class, also using Google Hangouts.
- **Eleventh grade**—Students exploring the stock market interview a financial advisor, stockbroker, or hedge fund manager to explore the

effect of stock prices on the economy. They ask the expert for permission to record their videoconference and incorporate the video into their final product, which they share with a partner class studying the same topic.

As someone who often conducts webinars and virtual professional development sessions with teachers, I know just how powerful it can be to broadcast ideas to hundreds of people from afar. At the same time, I always keep in mind that tasks must come before apps: finding a balance is important. The connections we create in real life are hard to replicate with digital tools, but technology has the benefit of connecting students with people and places that present logistical challenges to encounter in person. There is never going to be a single "right" approach because every situation is different—it is all about finding balance. Figure 4.5 shows how different tasks can be completed using a combination of digital and face-to-face communication.

Text-Based Correspondence

I remember as a student having to learn the intricacies of formatting different types of letters. Today, of course, students can simply find a template online to use and dedicate their energy to crafting a strong message.

Figure 4.5
Communicating On- and Off-Screen to Complete Tasks

Task	Digital Communication	Face-to-Face Communication
Create a movie that documents food's journey through the digestive system.	Students collaborate on a shared document to write a script and collect media outside school hours.	Students film the movie at school using a green screen app and editing software to create their video.
Visit a local bagel shop and learn about the economics of running a small business.	Students e-mail the shop owner to coordinate a visit and send a list of some initial talking points for the meeting.	Students visit the bagel shop to conduct their interview and tour the facility.

Although we no longer spend as much time teaching students how to write formal letters as we used to, the skills needed to clearly communicate have not disappeared.

Preparing students for digital text correspondence entails more than teaching them how to write an e-mail. Students today are corresponding through multiple channels, and they need to understand how to navigate a world where etiquette rules change depending on the digital context. When corresponding virtually with students for lessons or other reasons, take the time to impart lessons on digital citizenship and responsible communication. Modeling effective communication and sharing exemplars and nonexemplars with students can help facilitate these discussions.

Figure 4.6 shows examples of lessons that incorporate digital text correspondence.

Figure 4.6
Examples of Lessons That Incorporate Digital Text Correspondence

Type of Correspondence	Description	Lesson Example
E-mail	Message of any length sent through an e-mail provider; traditionally includes salutations; can be accessed on smartphones, tablets, and computers; may include attachments such as documents or images	Students send a formal invitation to a guest speaker or pose a question to an expert.
Text message	Short message (a single word to several sentences); sent primarily by phone over a cellular network	Students provide status updates to group members or use to coordinate group meetings.
Tweet	Message up to 140 characters long posted publicly to Twitter using a mobile app or web browser	Students pose questions or ask one another for clarification about an aspect of a project.
Facebook message	Message of any length sent to a Facebook account using a mobile app or web browser	Students send a message to a local organization asking about a potential site visit.

When folks outside of education think about technology in schools, they might picture 30 children staring into screens in a computer lab. These days, nothing could be further from the truth. Although devices and apps will change over time, the skills students need to make the most of technology tools will not. As we shift our thinking to prepare students for a world of unknowns, it is essential that students have opportunities to participate in collaborative tasks. It is our responsibility to ensure that students are ready to connect and communicate effectively in the real world as they tackle problems big and small.

5.

MOVING FORWARD
WITH PURPOSE

As we move from page to practice, I hope your wheels are spinning. Whether you have scribbled in the margins, filled in a graphic organizer with ideas, or circled a few strategies, it's time to take what you've learned and apply it to your classroom. In this chapter, we will work together to create a plan for moving forward. If you are reading this book by yourself, you can think of this chapter as a workbook of sorts, a place to jot down notes or draft your plan for getting started. If you are reading this book with a team, book club, or professional learning community, you can use the action steps and figures in this chapter to spark discussion or launch your next brainstorming session.

Choosing the Right Digital Tool

Placing *tasks before apps* means making learning front and center in your classroom. A video or a new digital tool might grab students' attention, but it's important to ensure that it addresses a specific learning goal or enhances a learning experience you have designed for students.

Check out a list of my favorite digital tools at http://www.classtechtips.com/tasksbeforeapps. If you'd like regular updates on my favorite tools and tips for teachers, sign up for my Weekly EdTech Roundup at http://www.classtechtips.com/signup.

Once you have a task in mind, how do you go about finding the perfect digital tool—say, an app that will let students record their voice to tell a story or a web browser–based tool that students can use to make movies? It's just as important to know *what* to look for as it is to know *where* to look. Searching for the perfect tool is easier when you have taken time to consider what your students need to be successful. Think about what you want your students to accomplish during an activity and consider the features they'll need to be successful (see Figure 5.1).

Action Step: Compose a Facebook post or send out a tweet asking for help locating a tool that meets the needs of your next project.

When it comes to deciding where to look for an appropriate digital tool, the options can feel overwhelming. There are blogs and websites dedicated entirely to reviewing and sharing new tools and old favorites. Teachers all over the world promote their favorite apps and devices on social media. Many educators organize their favorites into collections for others to make use of, too.

Figure 5.1
Choosing the Right Tool

If I Want My Students to . . .	I Need a Tool That . . .
Interview a family member	Records audio and is compatible with the tablets in our classroom
Watch a video clip	Scans a QR code or can access a link
Snap pictures on a community walk	Takes pictures and lets students upload them easily

I love creation tools that offer a range of possibilities for students, especially in a differentiated classroom. When I speak to groups of teachers about open-ended creation tools, I focus on choices that can be tailored to a wide range of tasks and across grade levels. As you review various creation tools, take special note of those with a multitude of features, as they can open up any number of possibilities. Consider using a checklist like the examples in Figure 5.2 as you conduct your search.

> **Action Step:** Use one of the templates in Appendix A to decide on the right tool for meeting your instructional goals.

Figure 5.2
Sample Tool Search Checklists

Name of Tool: Spark Page

Criteria	Yes	No	Notes
Makes it easy for students to access their work from anywhere	x		Student work is stored in the cloud and can be accessed from any web browser.
Requires a log-in	x		
Can be used on any device	x		Students can access their work from any device using a web browser (including their laptops) or the tablet/smartphone app.

Name of Tool: Book Creator

Criteria	Yes	No	Notes
Can be used to create an e-book	x		
Works on Chromebook laptops	x		
Allows for audio	x		Students can record their voice on every page.
Lets you change the font and text size	x		Great, because we have young readers.
Offers PDF exporting capability	x		

(Figure continues next page)

> **Figure 5.2**
> **Sample Tool Search Checklists** (continued)

Name of Tool: Google Slides

Criteria	Yes	No	Notes
Students can use the tool from home	x		Students will need their own log-ins.
Is completely free	x		
Lets students design slides for a presentation	x		
Includes project templates		x	I can create a project template and easily share it with students.
Allows for importing pictures	x		Students can use photos from their field trip.

Name of Tool: Spark Video

Criteria	Yes	No	Notes
Lets you download finished product as a movie file	x		This gives me the option to combine students' individual videos into one movie.
Lets you post the finished products online	x		I can share a link to student work on our school's Facebook page.
Allows for the target audience to view the finished products	x		There will be links to the videos so anyone with a smartphone, tablet, or computer can watch them.

Staying on Budget

Although I was fortunate enough to receive a set of iPad tablets to use with my 5th grade students, it was up to me to figure out which apps to use and how. One of the biggest challenges I faced was finding apps that were completely free. Many digital classroom tools offer both free and paid versions. I always recommend beginning with a free or trial version of a tool you've never used before to see if you really need the premium features.

Alternatively, your school might have one teacher per grade try out the full version of a tool to see if the extra features truly enhance teaching and learning.

When prioritizing resources, be sure to emphasize quality over quantity. It's possible that a single tool can address learning goals across subject areas or be used for multiple activities throughout the school year. For example, students could use a website creator tool like Spark Page to publish their investigations into endangered species in October and to share their pictures from a field trip in February. These are the kinds of tools you'll want to focus your energy on learning how to use. If you decide to invest in a digital tool with a price tag, like the powerful screencasting tool Explain Everything or the collaborative audio recording tool Soundtrap, you want to make sure you are making the best use of it.

> **Action Step:** Take stock of the resources available to you and your students. Jot down the types of digital devices students can use every day versus only occasionally.

Everyday Logistics

If students in your school are using shared devices, there are a few issues to keep in mind. For example, some apps and websites require students to log in with an e-mail or username and password. If the digital tool students use requires a log-in, they will be able to access their work on any device. For example, students who are logging in to their ThingLink account to create an interactive presentation do not need to sit at the same computer in the computer lab each day because they can log in to ThingLink on any web browser. On the other hand, when students are creating a movie or an e-book that saves all their work to the particular device they are using, they will need to remember that they used tablet #4 on Monday and check out the same tablet the next time they are working on their project.

> **The Children's Online Privacy Protection Act (COPPA)**
>
> When reviewing digital tools, you may notice that some mention their compliance with the Children's Online Privacy Protection Act (COPPA). This legislation was designed to ensure that parents retain control of any information that websites or apps collect from their children. It is due to COPPA that some digital tools are restricted to users over 13. You can learn more about COPPA at https://www.ftc.gov/tips-advice/business-center/guidance/complying-coppa-frequently-asked-questions.

Building Your Digital Tool Belt

Action Step: Next time you are touring the expo hall at a conference, snap a picture of a company's booth or its business card or flyer. Conferences can be overwhelming, and scrolling through pictures you snapped during the event can help you remember what digital tools caught your attention.

In this book, I have used the term *digital tool* to describe the mobile apps and websites students use to create and collaborate. These *tools* help students demonstrate their understanding of a topic and connect their learning to the real world. So it is only appropriate that we connect this term to a *tool belt*, a metaphor we can use to think about a growing list of favorite digital tools that enhance and energize learning experiences.

All teachers can build a tool belt with a set of go-to resources that address (1) learning goals, (2) differentiation needs, (3) device access, (4) infrastructure, and (5) teaching style (see Figure 5.3).

Figure 5.3
What Your Digital Tool Belt Should Address

Learning Goals	Differentiation Needs	Device Access	Infrastructure	Teaching Style
Meeting curriculum standards, developing transferable skills	Addressing the needs of special populations and individual students	How frequently the tool will be used and how many devices will be necessary to use it	The logistical necessities, such as the wireless access and tech support required by specific technology tools	How well the tool meets teacher and student comfort levels
What do I want students to do to demonstrate their understanding?	*What individual supports do my students need, and how will I address these needs with technology?*	*What devices do I have access to, and when can I use them?*	*What can I accomplish in my learning environment given the reality of certain logistical constraints?*	*What tool fits with my teaching style, and how will I stay motivated if something goes wrong?*

When a website gets a makeover and no longer fits your needs, or when an app that used to be free now charges for a subscription service, it can be easy to feel like you've wasted your time learning a new tool. Although tools may change over time, however, when you learn how to use a digital tool, the skills you and students develop are transferable to newer tools.

Figure 5.4 shows a selection of the tools I keep in my personal digital tool belt. I encourage you to type their names into your favorite search engine to locate the most up-to-date information about each one.

Gloriann Heikes, a 1st grade teacher from Minnesota, uses the tool Participate to keep all her media resources—including websites, videos, and apps—organized in one central place. Heikes also browses through collections from other Participate users to find specific resources on different topics. Because many of the curated items are vetted by Participate "Learning Advisors," she doesn't have to spend much time searching for the perfect tool.

Figure 5.4
Tools in Monica's Tool Belt

Name	Purpose	Similar Tools
Book Creator	Creating e-books with audio, text, video, and images	iBooks Author, Buncee
Spark Page	Creating a website with interactive features	Kidblog, WordPress
Google Docs	Creating collaborative documents students can use to connect and comment on one another's work	Microsoft Word, Pages
iMovie	Creating a movie that includes video, images, music, and narration	Spark Video, mysimpleshow
Explain Everything	Creating a tutorial using a screencast that captures audio, drawings, and annotation	ShowMe, Educreations
Seesaw	Creating an online space for recording and sharing videos, links, and pictures of student work	Drawp, Google Classroom

Goal Setting

The phrase *easier said than done* is a cliché for a reason. There are lots of great ideas for classroom instruction, but the ones that matter require us to go the extra mile. Let's explore how setting measurable goals and partnering with others can help you successfully incorporate digital tools into your teaching. Presenting goals in bite-size chunks can help us more realistically commit to them. Think about goals in terms of a week, month, or year:

> **Action Step:** Choose among the goal-setting templates in Appendix A to plan your short- and long-term goals related to technology integration.

- **Weekly**—Goals you can accomplish tomorrow or with just a day or two of preparation
- **Monthly**—Goals you may want to think about for a week or two, ask advice about from a colleague, or need some time to plan for
- **Yearly**—Overarching goals that may require long-term planning with colleagues or outside experts

Consider using a checklist like the one in Figure 5.5 to help with goal setting. In addition, the planning pages in Appendix A are designed to help you brainstorm what is needed to meet your goals.

Figure 5.5
Sample Goal-Setting Checklist

Guiding Questions	Answers
What is my goal?	To have students create tutorials for another 5th grade class explaining how to complete operations with fractions
What do I need to do to accomplish this goal?	• Find a screencasting tool. • Create an exemplar for students. • Design supports for students (e.g., a planning page or checklist). • Coordinate with another 5th grade teacher to share the student-created tutorials.
Where can I find help?	Search Pinterest or a favorite education blog for a screencasting tool or ask another teacher in the building for advice.
What is my plan if I get stuck?	Take a look at the screencasting company's website to see if there are any teacher stories showing this tool in action; ask for help during a Twitter chat for math teachers.
With whom can I share successes and obstacles?	At your next grade-level meeting, discuss some of the challenges of meeting this goal; send students' final products to the PTA president for posting on the school's Facebook page.

Finding a *Partner in Tech*

Working in a school with supportive, enthusiastic colleagues can make a hard day in the classroom so much easier. This is especially true when you are trying out new ideas and want to brainstorm with a fellow teacher. You may already have a go-to person in your grade level or department whom you turn to for advice—someone you always ask to join in when you try out something new. This same person could become your *partner in tech*—someone you work with to set goals for purposeful technology integration.

Sometimes it's hard to know whether you share the same goals as your colleagues. Reaching out to an administrator can be a great way to find peers who are ready to try something new. If there's no one in your school you feel comfortable inviting on your tech journey, many virtual communities exist that can act as support networks or simply places to gather ideas. One of my favorite places to go for both of these purposes is Twitter. When I first started using iPads in my classroom, I felt very isolated; I wasn't sure where to go to bounce off ideas. If it weren't for Twitter, finding information and connecting with like-minded teachers, my journey as an educator would have followed a much different path.

Fadé Ojeikere, an educator from Newark, New Jersey, has used Twitter and edcamps to build his professional learning network. He participates in CoffeeEDU events that bring local educators together once a month to talk about the work they are doing in their community. Events like edcamps and CoffeeEDU meetups can help you connect with passionate educators outside of your school building.

Action Step: Learn more about edcamp events in your community by visiting the Edcamp Foundation's website at http://www.edcamp.org.

Professional Learning Networks

You may have heard of the term *professional learning network*, or PLN. A PLN is a group of educators who come together to share ideas, obstacles, and success stories. Someone in this informal network may post an interesting article on his or her Facebook wall or ask colleagues a question on

Twitter. This virtual group of educators can push your thinking and provide ideas for you to explore.

So, how do you meet these powerful educators who are ready to help you on your journey? Participating in Twitter chats or joining online communities full of educators is a great place to start. Some education-focused websites have their own communities, or you can search within a tool you already use, like Facebook for Groups.

Action Step: Join my special Facebook group for educators sharing their EdTech journeys: https://www.facebook.com/groups/tasksbeforeapps.

Supporting Colleagues

If you're asked to share what you've learned after reading this book, attending a workshop, or participating in a conference, *where do you start*? Talking about what you've taken back and tried in your classroom helps you move from a good idea you've heard to a best practice with results that you can speak to. Sharing these experiences shows your colleagues that you have applied what you learned and can support them as they try out the strategies, too. An important part of sharing your experiences is embracing the struggle: if you've encountered an obstacle or anticipate a particular issue coming up, discuss it with your colleagues so they know you understand and appreciate when something new feels challenging.

Pinterest is a popular tool among educators. Not only do I use Pinterest boards to collect my favorite ideas for technology integration (see https://www.pinterest.com/class techtips), but I also use the site as a search engine by typing what I'm searching for at the top of the home page.

As a blogger and conference presenter, I love a good "Top Five" list. Presenting a list of a few favorite strategies is a great way to help other educators figure out what may work for them. Make sure to give your colleagues time to discover what suits their students' needs and their own teaching styles. Share five ideas that can help teachers address their learning goals; then let them explore each one and select the best fit. You may want to focus on strategies your colleagues can put into practice right away,

Action Step: Check out this list of popular Twitter chats for educators and choose one chat to join this month: https://www.participate.com/chats.

so they can build confidence and start demonstrating their own capacity for success.

Try to follow up with your colleagues after they've adopted a strategy to which you've introduced them. You might want to set aside a time for teachers to check in with you one-on-one or as a whole group to meet and discuss what they've implemented in their classrooms. As you talk about strategies with colleagues, remember that we all approach trying new things differently—some of us gingerly, others raring to go. Everyone's pathway as a learner is different, and this is no less true when we jump in and try new things in the classroom.

Action Step: Choose one strategy from this book to share with your grade level.

Action Step: Use the questions in Appendix B to guide a discussion around technology integration in a professional learning community or faculty meeting.

A FINAL NOTE

Dear Tech-Savvy Teacher,

You made it! You are now well on your way to designing engaging, meaningful tasks for students and choosing the right digital tools to support their learning journeys.

You've demonstrated a commitment to helping your students develop transferable skills so they are prepared for the unknowns of the future. You've brainstormed ways to bring this learning back to your classroom. Now it's time to get started! Use the checklists in Appendix A to begin. Don't wait—jump in. Then, share your story using the hashtag #TasksBeforeApps on Twitter, join our Facebook group to post a question, and invite a colleague to be your partner in tech as you put your goals into action.

This book will be here for you to reference and consult as a guide on your journey. Remember: the passion for teaching and learning that brought you to open up these pages will help you move through this week, this month, this year, and beyond as you work to place *tasks before apps*!

Yours in learning,
Monica

APPENDIX A: CUSTOMIZABLE PLANNING PAGES

Unit Planning

Unit Title: _____

Learning Goals: Students will be able to

1. _____

2. _____

3. _____

4. _____

Overarching Mission: _____

Culminating Task: _____

Expectation: _____

Technology Integration: Digital tools will be used to

- _____

- _____

- _____

- _____

- _____

- _____

Potential Tools:

- _____

- _____

- _____

- _____

The ACES Framework: Technology will elevate this unit by helping students to

- *Access* resources by _____

- *Curate* content by _____

- *Engage* with learning by _____

- *Share* with others by _____

Lesson Planning

Unit Title: _____

Unit Learning Goal Addressed in Lesson: _____

Description of Lesson: _____

Direct Instruction:

_____
_____
_____
_____
_____
_____

Group Exploration:

_____
_____
_____
_____
_____
_____

Teacher Tasks:

_____
_____
_____
_____
_____

The Lesson Addresses . . .

- *Creation:* _____
- *Curiosity:* _____
- *Collaboration:* _____

Survey Analysis Form

Unit Title: _____

Survey Questions:

    1. _____

    2. _____

    3. _____

Results:

_____

_____

_____

_____

_____

_____

_____

How will I incorporate this information into my unit?

_____

_____

_____

_____

_____

_____

_____

How will I use technology to further student interests?

_____

_____

_____

_____

_____

_____

Choosing the Right Tool

If I Want My Students to . . .	I Need a Tool That . . .

Tool Search Checklist

Name of Tool: _____

Criteria	Yes	No	Notes

Shared Device Checklist

Name of Tool: _____

Criteria	Yes	No	Notes
Lets students access their work from anywhere			
Requires a log-in			
Needs to be used on a single device			

Tools in My Tool Belt

Name	Purpose	Similar Tools

Overarching Goals

This Week	This Month	This Year

Content-Area Goals

Content Area	This Week	This Month	This Year

Class Section Goals

Class Section	This Week	This Month	This Year

Goal-Setting T-Chart

My Goals for the Year	What I Need to Meet My Goals

Goal-Setting Checklist

Guiding Questions	Example
What is my goal?	
What do I need to do to accomplish this goal?	
Where can I find help?	
What is my plan if I get stuck?	
With whom can I share successes and obstacles?	

APPENDIX B: DISCUSSION QUESTIONS

If you've picked up this book for a PLC or book club, use these questions to guide your discussion. Keep an open mind as you think through what strategies work best for your school, your teachers, and—most important—your students. Before you begin, consider the following three overarching questions:

1. Which big ideas resonated with you?
2. Which lesson examples seemed most feasible and relatable to you?
3. How would you like your classroom to evolve?

Creation

Reflection Questions

1. What products have students created this year?
2. Is there a task I designed that could be improved for students?
3. Do my project rubrics include content, creativity, and clarity?

Brainstorming Questions

1. How can I use creation tool features like audio or video to reach learners with different needs?
2. How can I use checklists and graphic organizers to support students during the creation process?
3. How can I use digital tools to make learning goals feel relevant for students?

Curiosity

Reflection Questions

1. Do I give students the time and space necessary to inquire about issues that interest them?
2. How have I sparked student curiosity?
3. Have I paused to monitor my students' evolving interests at different points in the school year?

Brainstorming Questions

1. How can I better connect tasks to student interests?
2. How can I use interest surveys to learn more about my students?
3. How can I incorporate both simple and deep-dive questions into student learning experiences?

Collaboration

Reflection Questions

1. What types of collaborative tasks have I designed this year?
2. Have my students participated in more than one collaboration model?
3. Do I give students enough opportunities for hands-on collaborative learning experiences?

Brainstorming Questions

1. How can I add a collaborative element to strengthen an activity from this year?
2. How can I incorporate digital citizenship skills into my lessons?
3. How can I leverage relationships with former colleagues, faraway educators, and content-area experts to connect students with collaborative partners?

Your Own Questions for Group Discussion

1.
2.
3.
4.
5.

REFERENCES

Anderson, L. W., & Krathwohl, D. R. (Eds.). (2000). *A taxonomy for learning, teaching, and assessing: A revision of Bloom's taxonomy of educational objectives.* New York: Pearson.

Blackburn, B. (2013). *Rigor is not a four-letter word* (2nd ed.). New York: Routledge.

Burns, M. (2016). *Deeper learning with QR codes and augmented reality: A scannable solution for your classroom.* Thousand Oaks, CA: Corwin.

Center for Media Literacy. (n.d.). *Media literacy: A definition and more.* Available: http://www.medialit.org/media-literacy-definition-and-more

International Society for Technology in Education. (2016). *ISTE standards for students.* Available: http://www.iste.org/standards

King, A. (1993). From sage on the stage to guide on the side. *College Teaching, 40*(1), 30–35.

Larmer, J., & Mergendoller, J. (2015). *Why we changed our model of the "8 essential elements of PBL."* Available: http://www.bie.org/object/document/why_we_changed_our_model_of_the_8_essential_elements_of_pbl#

Marzano, R. J. (2010). *Formative assessment and standards-based grading.* Bloomington, IL: Marzano Research Laboratory.

National Governors Association Center for Best Practices & Council of Chief State School Officers. (2010). *Common Core State Standards for English language arts.* Washington, DC: Author.

Partnership for 21st Century Learning. (2015). *P21 framework definitions.* Available: http://www.p21.org/storage/documents/docs/P21_Framework_Definitions_New_Logo_2015.pdf

Puentedura, R. J. (2014). *SAMR and Bloom's taxonomy: Assembling the puzzle.* Available: https://www.commonsense.org/education/blog/samr-and-blooms-taxonomy-assembling-the-puzzle

Renwick, M. (2016). *5 myths about classroom technology: How do we integrate digital tools to truly enhance learning?* Alexandria, VA: ASCD.

Robinson, K. (2006, June). *Do schools kill creativity?* Available: https://www.ted.com/talks/ken_robinson_says_schools_kill_creativity/transcript?language=en

Vitale-Reilly, P. (2015). *Engaging every learner: Classroom principles, strategies, and tools.* Portsmouth, NH: Heinemann.

Vygotsky, L. S. (1978). *Mind in society: The development of higher psychological processes.* Cambridge, MA: Harvard University Press.

Wagner, T. (2008). *The global achievement gap: Why even our best schools don't teach the new survival skills our children need—and what we can do about it.* New York: Basic Books.

Weinberger, D. (2011). *Too big to know: Rethinking knowledge now that the facts aren't the facts, experts are everywhere, and the smartest person in the room is the room.* New York: Basic Books.

Wiggins, G., & McTighe, J. (2011). *The Understanding by Design guide to creating high-quality units.* Alexandria, VA: ASCD.

INDEX

Note: Page references followed by an italiczed *f* indicate information contained in figures.

ABOUT
THE AUTHOR

Dr. Monica Burns is a curriculum and educational technology consultant, Apple Distinguished Educator, and founder of ClassTechTips.com. As a classroom teacher, Monica used one-to-one technology to create engaging, standards-based lessons for students. She has presented to teachers, administrators, and tech enthusiasts at numerous national and international conferences, including SXSWedu, ISTE, and EduTECH. She is a webinar host for SimpleK12 and a regular contributor to Edutopia. Monica is the author of *#FormativeTech: Meaningful, Sustainable, and Scannable Formative Assessment with Technology* (Corwin, 2017) and *Deeper Learning with QR Codes and Augmented Reality: A Scannable Solution for Your Classroom* (Corwin, 2016).

Monica visits schools throughout the United States to work with preK–20 teachers to make technology integration exciting and accessible. She also provides support to organizations using technology to reach children and families in need. Her mission is to help educators place *tasks before apps* and promote deeper learning with technology.

Visit ClassTechTips.com to find out more about working with Monica and her books and resources for educators.

Related ASCD Resources

At the time of publication, the following resources were available (ASCD stock numbers in parentheses).

PD Online® Courses
Enhancing Teaching with Technology (#PD16OC001M)

Technology in Schools: A Balanced Perspective, 2nd Edition
   (#PD11OC109M)

Print Products
5 Myths About Classroom Technology: How do we integrate digital tools to truly enhance learning? (ASCD Arias) by Matt Renwick (#SF115069)

Authentic Learning in the Digital Age: Engaging Students Through Inquiry by Larissa Pahomov (#115009)

A Better Approach to Mobile Devices: How do we maximize resources, promote equity, and support instructional goals? (ASCD Arias) by Susan Brooks-Young (#SF116020)

Learning Transformed: 8 Keys to Designing Tomorrow's School, Today by Eric Sheninger and Thomas C. Murray (#117034)

Teaching the 4 Cs with Technology: How do I use 21st century tools to teach 21st century skills? (ASCD Arias) by Stephanie Smith Budhai and Laura McLaughlin Taddei (#SF116038)

For up-to-date information about ASCD resources, go to **www.ascd.org**. You can search the complete archives of *Educational Leadership* at **www.ascd.org/el**.

ASCD EDge® Group
Exchange ideas and connect with other educators on the social networking site ASCD EDge at http://ascdedge.ascd.org/

ASCD myTeachSource®
Download resources from a professional learning platform with hundreds of research-based best practices and tools for your classroom at http://myteachsource.ascd.org/

For more information, send an e-mail to member@ascd.org; call 1-800-933-2723 or 703-578-9600; send a fax to 703-575-5400; or write to Information Services, ASCD, 1703 N. Beauregard St., Alexandria, VA 22311-1714 USA.